DEAD ELVIS

DEAD ELVIS

A Chronicle of a Cultural Obsession

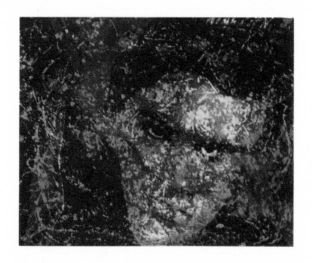

by Greil Marcus

DOUBLEDAY

NEW YORK   LONDON   TORONTO   SYDNEY   AUCKLAND

PUBLISHED BY DOUBLEDAY

a division of Bantam Doubleday Dell Publishing Group, Inc.
666 Fifth Avenue, New York, New York 10103

DOUBLEDAY and the portrayal of an anchor with a dolphin are
trademarks of Doubleday, a division of Bantam Doubleday Dell
Publishing Group, Inc.

FRONTISPIECE:

Mekons, *Portrait of Elvis Presley in the Style of Jackson Pollock*, No. 7,
laser origination by Chila Kumari Burman, 1989.

Previously published material is acknowledged on p. 213

Book design by Viola Adams

Library of Congress Cataloging-in-Publication Data
Marcus, Greil.
    Dead Elvis : a chronicle of a cultural obsession / by Greil
Marcus.
        p.   cm.
    Includes bibliographical references and index.
    1. Presley, Elvis, 1935–1977—Public opinion.
    2. Presley, Elvis, History and Criticism.
    3. United States—Popular culture.   I. Title.
ML420.P96M32   1991
782.42166′092—dc20
    [B]   91-10637
                                                               CIP
                                                               MN

ISBN 0-385-41718-7

for Dale and Steve Block

CONTENTS

INTRODUCTION

Elvis Presley's entry into public life came with such force his story was soon engraved into the cultural clichés that seemed to match it; the story became common coin because it already was. Birth in desperate rural poverty, a move to the city, a first record on a local label, unprecedented national and international fame, scandal, adulation; the transformation of a strange and threatening outsider into a respectable citizen who served his country without complaint, years spent dutifully making formulaic movies and unexciting music, marriage, fatherhood, a quiet life behind the walls of his mansion; then a stunning return, loud and vibrant; and then a slow, seemingly irresistible decline: divorce, endless tours as lifeless as his old films, news replaced by rumors of terrible things, and finally early death. The dates are familiar: 8 January 1935 for his birth, in Tupelo, Mississippi; 1954, for his first record, on the Sun label in Memphis; 1956, for his first appearance on the *Ed Sullivan Show*; 1968, for his comeback, on his own television special; 16 August 1977 for his death, at forty-two, at Graceland. The names are familiar: Vernon and Gladys Presley, his parents; Jesse Garon, the twin born dead shortly

Bar-min-ski (Bill Barminski), front sleeve of Death Ride '69 EP *Elvis Christ* (Little Sister), 1988.

before Elvis, buried in a shoebox in an unmarked grave; Sam Phillips of Sun, who produced his first singles; Colonel Tom Parker, his manager from almost the beginning to well past the end; Priscilla Beaulieu, the teenager he met in Germany while in the Army, whom he married in 1967, the mother of his daughter, Lisa Marie, born in 1968, his sole heir. We know it all.

But as Charles Wolfe, professor of English at Middle Tennessee State University, discovered in 1990 when he spoke to second and third graders at a mostly white, working-class public school in Jasper, Tennessee, there is another Elvis Presley, a figure made of echoes, not facts. "Do you know who Elvis Presley was?" Wolfe asked the children; though he found most of them confused as to whether the man was alive or dead, black or white, they did. "He was an old guy who was a king somewhere." "He was a great big man and he invented rock 'n' roll." "He lives in a big house in Memphis and he only comes out at night." "He's this big black guy who invented the electric guitar." "He was this guy who sang with his brothers Theodore and Simon"—a Chipmunk.

Between those Elvises are the Elvises I have followed since Elvis Presley's death. The enormity of his impact on culture, on millions of people, was never really clear when he was alive; it was mostly hidden. When he died, the event was a kind of explosion that went off silently, in minds and hearts; out of that explosion came many fragments, edging slowly into the light, taking shape, changing shape again and again as the years went on. No one, I think, could have predicted the ubiquity, the playfulness, the perversity, the terror, and the fun of this, of Elvis Presley's second life: a great, common conversation, sometimes, a conversation between specters and fans, made out of songs, art works, books, movies, dreams; sometimes more

Dave Abramson, collages from *Ahunka Lisa Marie* (Clambake Press), 1988.

than anything cultural noise, the glossolalia of money, advertisements, tabloid headlines, bestsellers, urban legends, nightclub japes. In either form it was—is—a story that needed no authoritative voice, no narrator, a story that flourishes precisely because it is free of any such thing, a story that told itself.

As a surprised, then amazed, then confused, finally entranced chronicler of this tale—in other words, simply someone who has paid attention to it—I am anything but its narrator. I have written sometimes as a critic, sometimes as a collector. Many voices speak in this book, often in images for which I've provided only captions and a context, often in streams of plain quotation, other people's words making cultural moments that need nothing from me. There is a good deal in this book I cannot explain. It's easy enough to understand a dead but evanescent Elvis Presley as a cultural symbol, but what if he—it—is nothing so lim-

Tony Fitzpatrick, *Memphis Tatoo King*, 1988.

ited, but a sort of cultural epistemology, a skeleton key to a lock we've yet to find? Certain questions occur again and again in these pages—in the conversation, in the noise, I've listened in on. Right from the start (or, if you like, the end), people asked, did Elvis go to heaven, or did he go to hell? *Everybody* asked, especially people who believed in neither, but who were having a great time fooling with the notion—and then the conundrum became a new language. As the story found its twists and turns, as it made a labyrinth, as it picked up speed, as it moved with the momentum of a flood in a mu-

Tattoo King

seum, strange creatures appeared: Elvis Christ, Elvis Nixon, Elvis Hitler, Elvis *Mishima*, Elvis as godhead, Elvis inhabiting the bodies of serial killers, of saints, fiends. Each was a joke, of course; beneath each joke was bedrock, obsession, delight, fear. Even as Graceland Enterprises, Inc., the corporation Priscilla Presley formed to market the legacy, gained increasing legal control over the image of Elvis Presley, its meanings spun further and further out of control. They cannot be controlled, any more than, in the beginning, Elvis Presley's body could stop moving; the shade of Elvis Presley is now an anarchy of possibilities, a strain of freedom less clear, but no less suggestive, than the man ever was.

In this book, then, the reader will not find commentary on whether Elvis Presley is, in the official sense, "still alive," on the exact cause of his death, on Elvis impersonators. This is a book about what Elvis Presley has been up to, in the last fourteen years: a small history of something much too big for one body, or one face. Elvis Presley made history; this is a book about how, when he died, many people found themselves caught up in the adventure of remaking his history, which is to say their own.

—GREIL MARCUS, BERKELEY,
1 APRIL 1991

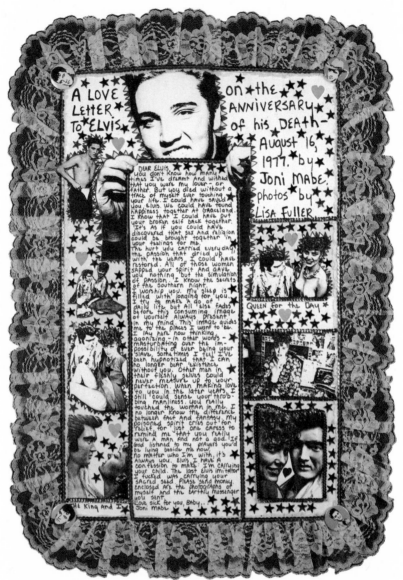

Joni Mabe, *Love Letter to Elvis*, 16 August 1983.

Blue Hawaii

1977

Blue Hawaii

AUGUST 18, MAUI, HAWAII   There was a message to call the main-
land, so I did. When we're here on vacation we don't follow the
news much. Especially on the outer islands, the radio is mostly
static; this trip we brought along a cassette machine and some
homemade tapes and didn't listen to the radio at all. "They want
you to write a piece about Elvis," I was told on the phone. "An
obituary." What kind of joke is that, I thought. *Rolling Stone* isn't
the *New York Times*, we don't keep obits on file. "What kind of
joke is that?" I said. "Why, he died today," I was told. "A heart
attack, apparently."

I didn't accept it at all, not in any way, but at the same time I
knew it was true, and even as part of me withdrew from that fact,
headlines began to fly through my brain. NUDE BODY OF GEORGE
"SUPERMAN" REEVES FOUND. SINGER DROWNS IN OWN VOMIT. JAMES DEAN
SPOKE TO ME FROM THE GRAVE, MAN CLAIMS. I went down to the bar
at the hotel where we were staying and ordered a Jack Daniel's,
straight from Tennessee, just like Elvis Presley's first 45s.

Like most other people my age—thirty-two—Elvis mattered to
me in the fifties; I loved his music, bought some of his records,
and never went to any of his movies. He was thrilling, but he was
also weird, and I kept my distance. Clearly, though, I had some
sort of buried fascination with the man, and when he appeared
on TV late in 1968 for his comeback, I found I could handle the
fascination. In fact I was caught up in it, and for the next five

2

years I spent far more time listening to Elvis's music, from the beginning on down, than to the music of anyone else. I found, or anyway decided, that Elvis contained more of America—had swallowed whole more of its contradictions and paradoxes—than any other figure I could think of; I found that he was a great, original artist; and I found that neither of these propositions was generally understood. So I wrote about it all, feeling, after twenty thousand words, that I had only scratched the surface.

I didn't write about "a real person"; I wrote about the persona I heard speaking in Elvis's music. I wrote about the personalization of an idea, lots of ideas—freedom, limits, risk, authority, sex, repression, youth, age, tradition, novelty, guilt and the escape from guilt—because they all were there to hear. Reading my responses back onto their source, I understood Elvis not as a human being (his divorce was interesting to me *musically*), but as a force, as a kind of necessity: that is, the necessity existing in every culture that leads it to produce a perfect, all-inclusive metaphor for itself. This, I tried to find a way to say safely, was what Herman Melville attempted to do with his white whale, but this is what Elvis Presley turned out to *be*. Or, rather, turned himself into. Or, maybe, agreed to become. And because such a triumph had to combine absolute determination and self-conscious ambition with utter ease, with the grace of one to whom all good things come naturally, I imagined a special dispensation for Elvis Presley, or, really, read it into the artifacts of his career: that to make all this work, to make this metaphor completely, transcendently American, it would be free. In other words, this would of necessity be a Faustian bargain, but someone else—and who cared who?—would pick up the tab.

I thought about all this, sitting at the bar, still believing what I'd written but wondering if I had not somehow turned myself into the most lunatic Elvis fan of all. Suddenly I began to get angry. I thought: DISGUSTING, SORDID, UGLY, SLEAZY, STUPID, WASTEFUL, PATHETIC. I thought of George Reeves again, another childhood hero, the way his death read off of the front page as a betrayal. I still could not make the event real. Every time I focused on it, the idea

3

of Elvis dead, *not here*, it seemed to imply that he had never been here, that his presence over twenty-three years had been an hallucination, a trick—and as a way to avoid the event, I began to glide toward the corpse. I got tough. I played journalist. No one could tell me he died of anything but booze and dope, I said to myself. Isn't that what everyone in showbiz dies from? Why should I think Elvis would be any different? Heart attack, my ass. I dumped the whole affair into Las Vegas. I wanted to cut loose from it all, to cut my losses, but I was still too angry, and confused, not at anyone or anything: not at Elvis, or myself, or "them," or the fans, or the media, or "rock 'n' roll," or success. It was simply rage. I was devastated.

The following night I watched two network television specials on Elvis's death. They were strange shows. On ABC one saw Chuck Berry, who has never hidden his bitterness at the fact that it took a white man to symbolize the new music Berry and others, Elvis among them, had created; here he didn't try to hide his satisfaction that he had lasted longer than "the King." "For what will Elvis be remembered among other musicians?" Berry was asked. "Oh," he replied, "boop, boop, boop; shake your leg; fabulous teen music; the fifties; his movies." Not a man you'd want to trade ironies with in a dark alley—but even Jerry Lee Lewis, the madman, the prodigal son of American music, had lasted longer. On the screen, one saw Elvis performing in Hawaii in 1973—we had been here at the time, too, and I remembered feeling like an idiot as I looked for him on the beach—and in this later incarnation Elvis even looked like George Reeves.

On the NBC special, hosted in an even tone by David Brinkley, a panel of experts had been assembled: Murray the K, the famous DJ, introduced, astonishingly, as the "first civilized person [i.e., Northerner] to play an Elvis record"; Steve Dunleavy, the as-told-to of a quartet of authors responsible for a just-published scandal-biography called *Elvis: What Happened?* (his cowriters were former Elvis bodyguards, fired over the last year or so); and Dave Marsh of *Rolling Stone*. Murray the K looked subdued and

4

played the insider: Elvis, he informed America, had told him, Murray, that he, Elvis, would "not outlive his mother," who, Murray said, had also died at forty-two (she was forty-four). Dunleavy looked bored, milked his Australian accent for all the British class it was worth, and spoke coolly of Elvis in his last years as "a walking drugstore." "It was a classic case of 'too much, too soon,'" he said, trying to slide around the cliché. Dave Marsh looked shell-shocked. He looked the way I was feeling, and he said things that perhaps not a large percentage of those watching were prepared to understand.

"It's that Elvis has always been there," Marsh said. "I always expected him to be a part of American culture that I would share with my children." And that was it. Elvis was not a phenomenon. He was not a craze. He was not even, or at least not only, a singer, or an artist. He was that perfect American symbol, fundamentally a mystery, and the idea was that he would outlive us all—or live for as long as it took both him and his audience to reach the limits of what that symbol had to say.

Since I had already read Steve Dunleavy's book, though, I could not help but think that Elvis's death might mean that those limits had already been reached, that the symbol had collapsed back on itself, and upon those who had, over the years, paid attention to it. The moment I'd enjoyed most in *Elvis: What Happened?* came when I read that in 1966 Robert Mitchum offered Elvis the lead in *Thunder Road*—a perfect role for Elvis, and one that could have given him the chance to become the serious actor he dreamed of being—and I enjoyed that moment most because I knew that Mitchum had made *Thunder Road* in 1958, and could so conclude that the accuracy of the rest of the book might be suspect. Because while many of the events detailed in *Elvis: What Happened?* are trivial ("The Most Unforgettable Pillow Fight I Ever Had"), and some of the most sensational clearly inflated (the tale of Elvis demanding that his bodyguards set up a hit on the man who took away his wife), what Red West, Sonny West, and Dave Hebler have to say rings mostly true.

The Elvis of *What Happened?* is a man whose success has driven him nuts. As presented here—in, of course, the present tense; the authors make much of their desire to save Elvis from himself; *it is not too late*, they say—Elvis has no sense of the real world whatsoever. He is schizophrenic, a manic depressive, insanely jealous, crazily "generous," desperate to buy loyalty and able to trust no one. Each of these horrors is intensified by huge and constant doses of uppers and downers, by an entourage of paid sycophants, by Elvis's obsession with firearms, and by his paranoid fantasies of vengeance and death. Each of these neurotic dislocations seeks resolution in Elvis's need to test the limits of what he can get away with (Can the near death of a young girl he overdosed be covered up? Sure it can) and in his desire to bring punishment upon himself for breaking rules he knows are right. Commentator after commentator on the night of Elvis's death mentioned that his life was never complete after his mother died, implying that had she lived he would have also; it seems clear, after reading *What Happened?*, that one root of Elvis's pathology was his inability—from, inevitably, the beginning—to be as good a boy as his mother must have wanted him to be.

I thought of this, however, only after Elvis's death; before that, I hadn't taken the book all that seriously. Now I realize that what I read in it was at the source of my anger at his death, my sense of ugliness and waste. The book disturbed me when I read it, but I merely wrote a brief review and forgot about it. It is only now that I can see through the padding and the mean-spiritedness of the thing to what it has to show us: a picture of a man who lived with nearly complete access to disaster, all the time. The stories that illuminate this reality are not particularly important: you can read them or you can make them up, whether they have to do with the onstage freak-out brought on by dope and who knows what else; the M16 that went off at the wrong time; the rage that no one could cool down. There is nothing in this book, I think, that would have ruined Elvis's career had he lived (perhaps today even the worst possibilities imaginable regarding Elvis's Army relationship with the then-fourteen-year-old Priscilla might not have really hurt him with Middle America; he did finally marry her, after all). But the book's last pages, purportedly the transcript of a telephone conversation between Elvis and Red West, occurring some time after Elvis fired him, a conversation in which they discuss the book that has come out as *What Happened?*, are ending enough.

The feeling I had, reading those last pages, was that Elvis may well have wanted the book to appear; that he wanted the burden and the glory of acting the King removed for good; that he wanted, finally, relief. Of course, that may only be what the authors of *What Happened?* want us to think. Peter Guralnick has written often about Elvis; almost every time, he has headed what he wrote with a quote from William Carlos Williams: "The pure products of America go crazy." In Elvis's case both Guralnick and Williams were obviously right. But it still seems too pat to me, as do the detailed explanations and apologies of *What Happened?* Both merely reduce something we cannot quite get our heads around to something that can be laid to rest by a line.

With Elvis in the ground his death is still out of my reach. This isn't, I know, just another rock 'n' roll death; it isn't any kind of rock 'n' roll death, because it is the only rock 'n' roll death that cannot be contained by the various metaphors rock 'n' roll has itself produced. Nor can it be contained, as Steve Dunleavy and, at times, I try to contain it, by showbiz metaphors. The problem— and it may take years to understand this, years during which some of us will have to keep the files straight and the stacks in order, reminding others that Elvis was not influenced by Chuck Berry, but by Roy Brown, and so on—is that there is just too much that has been dumped in our laps, and that all of it—the art, the boy, the man, the emergence in the South, the reward in Hollywood, the recognition and adulation all over the world for more than twenty years—is all mixed up together.

The problem is that Elvis did not simply change musical history, though of course he did that. He changed history as such, and in doing so he became history. He became part of it, irrevocably and specifically attached to it, as those of us who were changed by him, or who changed ourselves because of things we glimpsed in him, are not. And it must be added that to change history is to do something that cannot be exactly figured out or pinned down: it is to create and pursue a mystery. That Elvis did what he did—and we do not know precisely what he did, because "Milkcow Blues Boogie" and "Hound Dog" cannot be figured out, exactly—means that the world became something other than what it would have been had he not done what he did, and that half-circle of a sentence has to be understood at the limit of its ability to mean anything at all. Because of Elvis's arrival, because of who he was and what he became, because of his event and what we made of it, the American past, from the Civil War to the civil rights movement, from Jonathan Edwards to Abraham Lincoln, looks different than it would have looked without him. Because of that event, its moment—the mid-fifties—was convulsed, and started over. Because of that event, the future has possibilities that would have been otherwise foreclosed.

And you see, we knew all this. We knew it, I think, all the time. You can hear it in the music. Somehow, Elvis must have known it, too. That is why, really, his death makes no sense, no matter if he died of "an irregular heartbeat" (as the papers say today), an overdose, as a suicide, in an accident, or in any other way. And this is what, perhaps, Dave Marsh meant when he said that Elvis had always been there, and hinted that, at least for those of us who helped make Elvis's event, Elvis would of necessity have to outlive us. As with the death of FDR for another generation, it is not simply a person's death that makes no sense, and is in some crucial, terrible way not real. When history is personified, and the person behind that history dies, history itself is no longer real.

My wife came down to the bar and we talked about some of this while I watched the ice melt in my Jack Daniel's. She mentioned that she had asked me to tape Elvis's "Long Black Limousine," from the 1969 comeback album *From Elvis in Memphis*, for our trip; for some reason I had never gotten around to it. It is quite a song: the story of a country girl who goes off to make it in the city, sell her soul, and comes home, as she promised, in a fancy car—which turns out to be a hearse. Elvis never sang with more passion; he was bitter, and of what other recording by Elvis Presley can you say that? Of course, Elvis was no fool; he knew the song was about him, the country boy lost to the city if there ever was one, but he sang as if he liked that fact and loathed it all at once. He contained multitudes. His singing cut through the contradictions, blew them up. William Carlos Williams might say that the pure products of America go crazy, but you might also say that the crazy products of America are pure, or something like that. When the stakes are as high as they always were with Elvis, the neat phrase is not to be trusted; always, it will obscure more than it will reveal. So we talked about "Long Black Limousine," and about the only Elvis music we did have along, an outtake of "Blue Moon of Kentucky," from Elvis's very first sessions, in July of 1954, with studio dialogue bouncing back and forth between a nineteen-year-old Elvis, his accompanists Scotty Moore and Bill Black, and producer Sam Phillips. They were jammin' like crazy, they said. And they were.

We sat for a while longer, and I ordered another Jack Daniel's. My wife explained the rationale to the bartender, who seemed amused. There was, he said, a much more appropriate drink. We asked what. "Why," he said, "a Blue Hawaii. You know, the movie?" That was two nights ago, but I still haven't been able to bring myself to try one.

Illustration from unknown pop music newspaper, Morocco, about 1970.

Pre-Dead Elvis

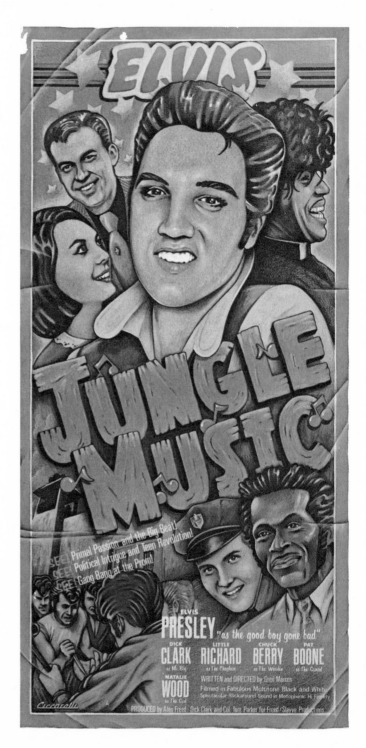

Gary Ciccarelli, illustration for
"Jungle Music," *Creem*, July 1975.

1975

Jungle Music: The All-Time All-Star 1950s Rock 'n' Roll Movie

STARRING

Elvis Presley
as the Good Boy Gone Wrong

Gene Vincent
as the Bad Boy Gone Wrong

Fats Domino
as The Old Con

Pat Boone
as The Prison Guard

Little Richard
as The Chaplain

Chuck Berry
as The Warden

Jerry Lee Lewis
as The Leader of the Pack

Frankie Lymon, Ritchie Valens, Dion,
the Del-Vikings, the Everly Brothers,
and Many Others
as Members of the Pack

Buddy Holly
as The Leader of the Laundromat

Carl Perkins, Rod McKuen, Frankie
Avalon, Frankie Sardo, the Platters,
the Three Chuckles, and Many Others
as Members of the Laundromat

Bo Diddley
as The Dean of High Hopes High School

Fabian
as The Dope Pusher

Dick Clark
as Mr. Big

Eddie Cochran
as The Undercover Agent

Natalie Wood
as The Girl

and featuring
Alan Freed
as President of the United States

FADE IN   on a crowded country music bar. Alone on the band-
stand, Elvis Presley is singing "Don't Be Cruel." Halfway through
the number a drunk staggers to the stage and vomits on Presley's
blue suede shoes. Elvis smashes the man with his guitar; suddenly

the room is in chaos. Several goons jump Elvis; the lights go out. We can barely make out Gene Vincent, dressed in black from head to foot, as he flicks open a knife and plants it square in the back of one of Elvis's assailants. As the crowd scatters, the lights go up; the police arrive. No one is left in the bar but Presley, Vincent, and the corpse. The police handcuff the two young men and lead them away.

High Hopes High School. On the soundtrack: "High School Confidential." The Pack, led by Jerry Lee Lewis, and the rival Laundromat, led by Buddy Holly, are in the midst of a lunchtime face-off over Natalie Wood, the only girl in school. The Pack make quick work of the Laundromat and are moving in on Wood when Dean of Boys Bo Diddley appears on the scene. "More small potatoes," Bo sneers at Jerry Lee. "I always said the Pack ain't got no class." Nettled, Jerry Lee rolls Holly's unconscious body down a flight of stairs. "How's that, Dean Diddley?" Jerry Lee asks politely. "That's *class*, man!" smiles the Dean; Natalie Wood takes Jerry Lee's arm and gazes at him adoringly. Soundtrack: "I Only Have Eyes for You."

The State Prison. Warden Chuck Berry is at his desk. "Thirty years, thirty years," he sings to himself. "Gonna take you thirty years to get back home." Guard Pat Boone enters. "Time to sign out Fabian," Boone reports. "The Parole Board ordered him freed today." " 'Bout time," snaps Berry. "Payoff came through from Mr. Big months ago. I'se beginning to worry we was gonna have to give it *back*."

The prison exercise yard. Soundtrack: "Rock Around the Rockpile." "Dadgummit!" Vincent whines. "Why'd that creep Fabian get sprung?" "I'm sure I don't know," says Elvis. "Must be God's will."

"God's will, my aunt," says Vincent. "He's out, we're *in*. I'm going nuts in here! I'm gonna blow! We'll never get out! Never!"

"Ain't that a shame," calls a voice; Elvis and Vincent turn to

15

see Fats Domino lumbering across the yard. "Who're *you*?" Vincent growls.

"They call me the Fat Man," Domino says, " 'cause I weigh two hundred pounds. All the boys love me 'cause I know my way around, and I know why Fabian's on the street. Mr. Big's slipping *payola* to Warden Berry, that's why. Mr. Big's sending Fabian down to High Hopes High School to hook the whole student body on dope, and everybody from the Warden to the High Hopes Dean got a piece of the action!"

"That's *terrible*," says Elvis. "I figured that Fabian for a ringer ever since I heard him sing 'Hound Dog Man' at the prison variety show. We gotta save those kids—and maybe get ourselves a pardon in the bargain."

"Reet petit, King," Vincent says. "I suppose we just ask Buck Cherry for a pass and waltz on out, so's we can queer his scam?"

"God will show the way," Elvis says.

"Darn straight," says the Fat Man. "You know crazy Richard, the chaplain? Well, he's always looking for converts, and he's blackmailed the Warden into letting a couple out each month for a night so he can take 'em up to his Holiness church and get 'em born again. But—you gotta learn how to speak in tongues."

"I already know how," Elvis says.

"*Fine*," says the Fat Man. "You just stay cool. Wait til Richard gets into his stuff and the place is going wild, sneak out, double back to High Hopes High. It's a cinch. But remember, you gotta act *devout*. That Richard may be crazy, but he can tell the wheat from the chaff like Mr. Big can tell horse from sugar."

A small wooden church filled with a screaming mob. Richard stands at the pulpit chanting, picking up momentum by the second. "TUTTI FRUTTI!" he shouts. "ALL ROOTIE! I'M READY! I'M READY READY READY TO ROCK 'N' ROLL RIGHT INTO THE ARMS OF THE LORD! I DON'T WANT NO UNCLE JOHNS JUMPIN' BACK IN THE ALLEY TO*NIGHT*! I DON'T WANT NO LONG TALL SALLY, I DON'T WANT NO MISS ANN! I WANT—"

Elvis and Vincent stand facing the pulpit, draped in white. The congregation begins to sanctify; then lightning strikes the church and plunges it into darkness. "Now!" whispers Vincent. He and Elvis turn to escape, but a huge blue flame materializes behind Richard; he raises his arms toward the roof and begins to scream. Elvis, his face bathed in the blue light, is transfixed.

Shifty, Vincent says, "For heaven's sake, nobody's looking now, let's make our break!"

Elvis smiles and says, "Nix, nix. I gotta—"

"NOW I'M REALLY READY!" Richard howls. Vincent knocks Elvis over the head with a hymnal and drags him from the church as the worshippers go into hysterics. "I'M READY READY READY READY READY . . ."

Quick cuts of Fabian, Elvis, Vincent, and a new face we recognize as Eddie Cochran, all registering as transfer students at High Hopes High. Soundtrack: "School Is In."

The screen reads TWO WEEKS LATER. Study Hall. The Laundromat, with Fabian in their midst, are nodding off, falling over, and laughing madly. Fabian has made his first connection. At the other end of the room sit the Pack, with new members Elvis, Vincent, and Cochran. "What's *happening?*" says Jerry Lee to his boys. "I know," says Elvis brightly. "It's that little Fabian who—"

"*Cool it!*" Cochran hisses. "Meet me after school. We gotta talk. But *cool it.*"

Cochran, Elvis, and Vincent are huddled in a booth in the Soda Shop. "All right," snaps Eddie. "I got something to spill. I wasn't supposed to cop, but I gotta if I'm gonna keep you guys in line. *I'm not really a student here.*"

"Well, kiss the moon," sneers Vincent.

"We're not *either*," glows Elvis. "We're here to nab Fabian and Mr. Big and save the kids!"

"And *us*," Vincent adds.

"That's really *something else*," says Eddie, flashing a badge. "I'm Treasury. What's your outfit?"

17

"Uh, freelance," says Vincent.

"As it happens," Cochran says. "I don't care what your cover is. But here's the story so far. We can't move on Fabian til we flush Mr. Big into the open, and by that time he's gonna have the whole school on the needle. We don't even know who he is. We need a plan."

Elvis notices Vincent and Cochran tapping their fingers to "Race with the Devil," playing on the jukebox. "Do you dig the Rock?" Elvis asks. " 'Cause if you do, we just might form a band—everyone knows musicians are junkies—and Mr. Big will come to *us*. And even if he doesn't, we can pick up some bread playing the prom. You go for it?"

Vincent and Cochran look to Elvis with stunned admiration. "We need a name," Eddie says after a long moment. " 'The Go-Valeers'?"

" 'The Plume Gods'?"

" 'The Wrong Way'?"

" 'The Vacant Lot'?"

" 'The Last Period'?"

Elvis gets a gleam in his eye. "How 'bout—'The Rolling Stones'?"

"I like it," says Vincent. "I like it *a lot*. It *says* something."

"What?" says Elvis.

"OK, Stones!" Eddie cries. "Let's shake it!"

Prom night at the High Hopes gym. Students wander the room in a daze, not even bothering to hide the works in their pockets. Off to one side the Pack and the Laundromat are taking on Natalie Wood one by one, while Dean Diddley administers injection after injection to the nearly comatose girl. "Help me, Jerry Lee," she moans; he giggles like a moron. Fabian snakes through the crowd, keeping the supply up, occasionally snorting from a glassine envelope. The Pack and the Laundromat turn Natalie over to Dean Diddley while passing a dirty needle from hand to hand, splattering each other's clothes with junk. Elvis, Eddie, and Vincent gather backstage.

"*Great* idea, King," Vincent mutters. "We got the band, we got the gig, we ain't got Mr. Big, and any minute people are gonna start wondering why we're the only ones in school without tracks on our arms." "Keep your sleeves rolled down and your head straight," Elvis says; they hit the stage. They run through three furious tunes—"Hound Dog," "Summertime Blues," and "Be-Bop-a-Lula." Not one High Hoper plays the slightest attention; Mr. Big is nowhere to be seen. The plan has failed. Broken, the Stones head backstage.

There, waiting for them, is Dick Clark.

"Hi, I'm the world's oldest teenager," he says. "I've heard about you boys. I like your sound. We can go places. I can make you."

The Stones forget their mission, Fabian, Mr. Big, prison. They see records, stardom, money, girls: the American dream.

"We're ready," says Elvis.

"We want the big time," says Vincent.

"Where do we sign?" says Cochran.

"Great," says Clark. "Let's shoot on it."

Immediately it hits them. This is Mr. Big. The whole school has gone under and only they are left. Today, High Hopes—tomorrow, High School U.S.A. *Dope School U.S.A.* Their dreams of glory fade on their faces; they have no choice. One wink between them and they take Mr. Big without a struggle.

With Fabian, Dick Clark, and Dean Diddley in chains, and the students entering the first stages of cold turkey, Eddie puts in a call to Washington. "We got him, Chief," he says to President Alan Freed. "But I'm through. I want a pardon for my friends, and then we're going on the road. I want a clean life, sir—I'm tired of messing with scum. From now on, it's rock 'n' roll for me."

"Congratulations, son," says the President. "I know the kids just love that jungle music. Good luck—you'll need it." Then his voice grows hard. "But you better remember one thing, and that goes double for your pals."

"What's that, President Freed?" asks Eddie.

"I had half a mil tied up with Mr. Big, you little twerp, and you blew it for me, you and your bopcat buddies. I never dreamed you'd turn down his offer. So go on, rock around the clock, slop til you drop, shake til you break. I could care less. But you make sure my office gets half of every gig, and every cent of your publishing—or the only groove you'll get into will be six feet in the ground."

The phone clicks dead. Elvis and Vincent look hopefully at Eddie, anxious to hear the results of the call. Slowly, Cochran turns toward them.

A look of incredible horror is on his face.

FADE OUT

THE END

1975

King Death

In Tupelo, Mississippi, an Englishman gazes idly from his hotel window. His eye is caught by two men on the street below. One seems to pass through the other. The Englishman realizes that the man who passes through is a hired killer, and that he who is passed through is, was, his victim. The tableau unfolds repeatedly in the Englishman's mind. The clarity, the delicacy of the act—never has he seen anything to compare with this moment.

That evening the Englishman spots the killer in a bar. He approaches him; they discuss the philosophy of death. The Englishman is permitted to accompany the killer on his next mission. Again he is overwhelmed. He makes a proposition.

I am a producer, he tells the killer. I have long since conquered Hollywood. I thought I had reached the limits of my art. Yet you are the noblest performer I have ever seen. Giving death, you give grace to your victim, who becomes, for a holy instant, your supplicant. I will make you the greatest star the world has ever known. All will then comprehend the unspeakable glory of death, for together we will show it to the masses as you have shown it to me.

And so it comes to pass—or rather Nik Cohn pulls it off. He begins his novel *King Death* with this improbable and somewhat shlocky premise, and fashions from it an elegant fiction that has the queer conviction of a waking dream and the crazed unreality of pop culture itself.

Despite his endless pledges to the pop creed of fun fun fun, most obviously in his history *Pop from the Beginning*,* Cohn has always been intrigued by the thanatology of pop—in his novel *I Am Still the Greatest Says Johnny Angelo*, in his conception and framing of Guy Peellaert's paintings in *Rock Dreams*. Here he is beginning at the beginning. It is no accident that his killer comes out of Tupelo; he is, Cohn implies in the book's dedication, the other half of the grandest pop hero of all. King Death is the risen ghost of Jesse Garon Presley, Elvis's still-born twin.

This is more than Cohn's little in-joke. Nearly all novelists who take pop music as their subject exploit the repressed violence and death wishes that seem to lie behind the ecstasy of pop thrills; in *King Death* Cohn goes beyond the usual apocalyptic ending (where the star's big concert closes with an orgy of mayhem, murder, and even cannibalism), making the underside of the story the story itself. If oblivion is what the mass psychology of pop is all about, why fool around? Death, reasons Cohn's producer, is what the people want in their hearts. What could be more satisfying, for an artist, than to give it to them?

In Cohn's wonderful phrase, the producer "buys all rights" to a group of families, turns them into a captive audience for his new property and, testing one scenario against another, persuades America to kneel before the Tupelo hit man as before a god, every week on prime time. If as social theory the process by which this triumph is achieved is a load of overheated British fantasy, as a tight little horror story it is all too convincing.

As the book nears its end—an ending implicit in the deal first struck between the producer and the killer—you get the feeling Cohn is less telling the tale of King Death than, like his producer, promoting him. Cohn blasts that thought in a final scene far more chilling than any of the action that has preceded it.

With *King Death*, though, Cohn has taken his vision of pop as far as it can go; there can be no follow-up. But such a dead end fits Cohn's vision perfectly. In his world, performers are supposed

22   * Later republished as *Awopbopaloobop Alopbamboom*.

to dry up and disappear when their work reaches a self-consuming conclusion, or when they hit thirty. Which raises the question: where is Elvis in this story?

Front sleeve of Jesse Garon & the Desperadoes EP *The Adam Faith Experience* (Velocity, U.K.), 1987.

Cover of *National Examiner*, 4 October 1988.

The Absence of Elvis

1981

Elvis: The Ashtray

In 1981 I was invited to speak at the third annual Salute to Memphis Music, held as it had been the previous years at Memphis State University on August 16, the anniversary of Elvis Presley's death. Given the location, I misunderstood the forum; I expected an academic symposium, with an audience of teachers and students. Instead there were testimonials and reminiscences from those who had known the King—friends, relatives, his dentist's wife—and one speaker from elsewhere. The audience was mostly Southern, white, middle-aged, and working class.

I had two props. I ran a video of Elvis's performance of "Tryin' to Get to You" from his comeback television special; as the crowd on the video burst into wild applause, so did the crowd in Memphis. I brought out an Elvis whiskey bottle, twisted off the head, and poured bourbon—Missouri bourbon, of all things—out of the neck and into a glass.

That was Elvis in 1968, facing an audience for the first time in nine years; and that was Elvis today, four years after his death. Nobody, I think, knows what to make of this: the singing and the bottle. The contradiction is too big. Contrasts and contradictions have always been the language in which Elvis has been talked about: the polite rebel, the gospel rocker, the country boy in Hollywood. True folk artist and commodity fetish. Clean living model for the nation's youth with his own drugstore. Why, said the promoter, with this boy I could reach—everyone.

26 Even in that video of Elvis sitting on stage with Scotty Moore

and D. J. Fontana, reinventing his music on the spot—the performance is about an hour long, we saw only a favorite moment—there's a contradiction. Elvis laughs while drawing the deepest passion out of himself: that's no contradiction. He merely removes a bit of the edge from a performance almost too powerful to grasp all at once—removes the edge for himself, and for us. It takes him a while to get warmed up, the first few numbers are formal run-throughs or self-parodies, but once Elvis takes the electric guitar from Scotty Moore and begins to lead the music, we're in a new world. To take a line from Albert Werthheimer, a photographer who traveled with Elvis in 1956, responding to this music isn't a matter of taste, it's a matter of whether you're a living, breathing human being. But then Elvis sets down the guitar. Strings come up, and he puts on a solemn face. He walks to the edge of the little stage, raises a hand mike, and begins to sing a song called "Memories."

It's a rotten song: funeral music. Worse than that: music for a commercial advertising a mortuary. Elvis, naturally, sings with true reverence. What the performance says is this: What I just did (I didn't know I had it in me), what you just saw (you didn't think I had it in me), wasn't real. It might have been the greatest music of his life, it might be a central moment in the history of American culture—but we'll chalk it up to nostalgia. Memories. Fifties stuff, the old songs. Remember where you were when you first heard Elvis sing "Tryin' to Get to You" like that? Forget that you can't remember where you were when you first heard Elvis sing "Tryin' to Get to You" like that—he never did before, and he never did again.

"They're going to let me do what I want," Elvis says at the beginning of the performance, talking like a prisoner out on parole. Later, he tells the crowd there's time for only one more song; another audience is coming in. The crowd doesn't boo, but they let him know they're disappointed. "Hey, I just work here," Elvis says. Then he hoists the guitar again and sings rhythm and blues—and offers a metaphor for the possibilities of life that makes almost every job, every love affair, every religious experience, every pres-

27

idential candidate—save, perhaps, Franklin Roosevelt—seem like a shoddy compromise.

What I'm getting at is this: Elvis was too big, too complex— too much—for any of us to quite take in, to see all at once, to understand. He was too big, finally, for us to live with. To use a psychological term, he was too big for us to incorporate into ourselves. He confounds us. Like Medusa, you can't look at him head on. So we look sideways. From one angle, we see the young man who untangled and rewove the strands of American identity with "Good Rockin' Tonight"; from another angle, we hear that same young man declare Kay Starr his favorite female singer—insisting, in not so many words, that such an image of American identity, fixed and sterile, will do just fine. We may not be comfortable with such a contradiction, but what we're truly uncomfortable with, I think, is bigger still: the possibility that this is no contradiction at all. Millions of people found comfort precisely in this contradiction: without it, they wouldn't have been comfortable with the Elvis who got into fights, who did a bump and grind on stage, who sang "Hound Dog."

As long as Elvis was alive—as long as there was still some possibility of a resolution to his career—some last confession, perhaps, or some unheard, unknown, unimaginable musical synthesis—this was fascinating, but it wasn't exactly a problem. Sure, I may be making too much of Elvis singing a stupid, life-denying tune only seconds after singing a tune I think would do as a version of life itself: this was, we can say, just a touch the producer added. It had nothing to do with the *real* Elvis. "I just work here," he says—but what does *that* mean? This moment was planned, it was in the script, and we can say what counts is what happened during those moments that couldn't be planned, that couldn't be scripted, and we saw what happened then. That kind of talk was good enough, some years ago. But now we seize on smaller things, we try to find meaning in them, because Elvis's story, and his music, is at times so grand, so unsettling, and we're desperate to understand. Some part of us is wrapped up in some part of Elvis Presley. What part? What happens? What happens is what critic

28

Paul Nelson said happened with Bob Dylan: "People would search through his trash, his dropped cigarette butts, looking for a sign. The scary thing is, they'd find it."

It's troubling; we can't ever understand. Elvis's story has been told again and again, the litany of his success and failure has been recited until it seems like an old blessing and an older curse, and the tale explains everything but what we want to know: how did he do that? Why did I respond? Freud lets us off the hook. Halfway through his psychobiography of Leonardo da Vinci—after pinning down da Vinci's vulture fantasy, after explaining why da Vinci painted what he painted, why he designed his flying machines— even after explaining the reasons behind the *way* da Vinci painted his paintings and designed his flying machines—after all that, Freud said, now we come to the question of genius. In other words, okay, paintings; all right, flying machines. But why so profound? Well, Freud said, we all know genius is incomprehensible.

This is part of the problem with Elvis. Yes, he was a genius, but not the kind we're accustomed to. Was he even an artist? He didn't even write his own songs. So we listen to writers and news analysts—the people who turned up on television when Elvis died—tell us that if Elvis hadn't brought together white country music and black blues, and thus changed the contours and the symbolism of American life, changed the symbols by which we interpret our culture to ourselves, interpret what it means to be American, then someone else would have done the same. It's in the momentum of history, we're told; in 1954, the very year the Supreme Court ruled racial segregation unconstitutional, it was in the cards. But you can listen to every proto-rockabilly singer— to some very good ones, like Roy Hall, who one day sat down with a black friend and wrote "Whole Lotta Shakin' Goin' On," and recorded one of the first versions of that song—and what you hear in Elvis simply isn't there. You can listen to Jimmie Rodgers and Hank Williams, both originals, neither of whom would have existed without the blues, and it isn't there. You can listen to Elvis at the very beginning and it is there; you just can't tell what it is. All the sociological and musicological explanations about Elvis's boyhood and his background and his taste and his favorite radio stations won't explain it. You can go right to the edge, and then it all vanishes.

America is a young country, as countries go. Because of that, and because it's a polyglot country, filled with people of all sorts, made out of a clash of languages and regions and religions, and because it's based in crime, in slavery and the extermination of the Indians, and because it's based in a war, the Civil War, a war that has yet to be fully settled, we're uncertain about what it is to be American—uncertain, and eager for a nice, neat definition. There have been a lot of them, some enforced by law and some set forth in poetry. This is our great subject, but of late it's been narrowed down, as if we've given up on the question, on our story.

Ray Ginn, cover of *The Future Looks Bright Ahead*, cassette anthology of Southern California punk bands (Poshboy), 1981.

Now we ask, what does it mean to be a black American? A white Southern American? An Italian American? A Jewish American? We're relatively comfortable with these questions. But if we chance to encounter a figure like Herman Melville, or Abraham Lincoln, Emily Dickinson, William Faulkner, Howlin' Wolf, or Elvis Presley, they blow those neat questions apart.

For some years now, I've thought of Elvis in terms of blues singers like Robert Johnson and punk bands like the Sex Pistols or X— the Los Angeles group that's just put out a tune called "Back 2 the Base," the best song about Elvis since Bill Parsons' "The All American Boy"—and I've thought of Elvis in terms of Melville and Lincoln and Faulkner. Some people have been interested in the notion of looking at Elvis this way, and some people have been irritated, but what has actually upset people is the argument that Elvis belongs in this company because he was, in a way that we don't quite understand, conscious. He knew what he was doing. If he redefined what it means to be American, it was because he meant to. He wanted change. He wanted to confuse, to disrupt, to tear it up. He was not, in any important manner, a folk artist, as RCA once called him and as timid folk have called him ever since—he was not an exemplar of "the people." Watch him as he first appeared on television in 1956, watch the way he moves, what he says, how he says it: the willfulness, the purpose, is unmistakable. And yet so many of us missed it: as we watched, we drew a veil over the man bent on saying what he meant.

It wasn't only the idea of the conscious actor that led me to place Elvis and Lincoln and Melville together, though—it was as much the sense of mystery in the speeches, the novels, the music. No one knows how to explain the grace in Lincoln's Second Inaugural Address. No one knows how to explain the unholy power of the chapter in *Moby-Dick* called "The Whiteness of the Whale," the chapter that makes you wish that you too were on the ship, on the hunt. And no one knows how to explain the music I showed on the video. "I don't get it," a musician friend said of Elvis's guitar playing, as we watched that video a few weeks ago. "Those are such easy chords."

With each of these examples there is a presentation, an acting out, a fantasy, a performance, not of what it means to be American—to be a creature of history, the inheritor of certain crimes, wars, ideas, landscapes—but rather a presentation, an acting out, a fantasy of what the deepest and most extreme possibilities and dangers of our national identity are. We read, or we listen, or with Lincoln we read and we imagine ourselves listening, then and there, on the spot, and we gasp. We get it. We feel ennobled and a little scared, or very scared, because we are being shown what we could be, because we realize what we are, and what we are not. We pull back.

We can't explain, but we can explain away. Melville was not much talked about until the 1920s, but after that he slowly became an academic industry, and his best books have stood up against the shallowest and the most pretentious analysis. The *TV Guide* listing for the film of *Moby-Dick* provides all the summation that's really necessary: "An American epic in which the mad captain of a whaling ship chases a white whale." That's enough for us to respond to. Lincoln has been an enigma, a saint, and a reproach ever since he was made a martyr. Faulkner took the curse of the Civil War upon himself and watched as his characters struggled to escape it, which he never permitted them to do. And yet each of them has been whittled down; a great attempt has been made to make these people, and their legacies, manageable. Melville? Central figure of the nineteenth-century American literary renaissance. Lincoln? Keeper of our national soul. Faulkner? Mississippi's truest voice.

The same thing is going to happen to Elvis. It's already happening; the process is well advanced. There is less mystery every day. To many people, Elvis was no sort of creator, just an uneducated country boy with a smart manager and a gullible, thrill-seeking public to exploit. There's no aura of genius, of mystery, surrounding him; the very idea is ludicrous. To many who revere Elvis, the absence of genius is just as vital: their Elvis is a kind of innocent, passive, a hero because of where he came from and where he went. His death adds a layer of guilt to the story—Elvis's guilt, and the guilt of those who loved him but could not save him—and so this image is very powerful, a closed, imploding circle. To other Americans, Elvis is just a name, a joke, a few scandals. Or he is a symbol of rebellion. Or he existed only in 1954 and 1955, when he recorded for Sun Records here in Memphis, before he was swallowed up and spit out by big business and mass culture. To say that this last idea of Elvis ignores most of his music, its complexity and its contradictions, the seeming gap I began with, is no strong criticism: all of these ideas of Elvis ignore most of his music, as each denies every other. In every case, a piece of Elvis for Everyone, and no effort to discover why an everyone even comes into play, no attempt to seek out the whole story, to take it on its own terms, to say what those terms might be.

People have always talked about the real Elvis. We have a reason for attempting to find the real Elvis on tape, on the video we watched, or we have a motive in the invisible but undeniable connection between the video and the bottle. But as the bottle says, the real Elvis now seems more than anything else a question of marketing. There is an audience out there, right here: find it, map it, service it, use it up. The idea of Elvis as a market is the idea that Elvis *can* be used up. What have we seen, then, since Elvis's death? What do we see as the market brings him down to size?

One result of Elvis's death was a lot more to hear and a lot more to watch. Videos like the one we saw, at first pirate tapes, now official products available anywhere. Scores of new records, most of them bootlegs of very early live shows, TV appearances, dozens of later concerts, even of the famous Million Dollar Quartet sessions from 1956. Almost secret albums containing the talk that went on in the Sun studio between Elvis, Sam Phillips, and Scotty Moore when the first songs were cut. Endless repackagings of recordings already issued. But this is for a relatively small legion of fans, not for the country itself. The country itself is aware of something very different: of Elvis as an emptied, triumphantly vague symbol of displaced identity.

The country is aware of Elvis as a weird icon: as a T-shirt, a black velvet wall hanging, an emblem of working-class bad taste or upper-class camp, an ashtray, a $200 baby doll with a porcelain head marked down to $125, a commemorative limited-edition dinner plate. The country is aware of Elvis as he's been worshipfully caricatured by thousands of Elvis imitators, and sneering imitators of Elvis imitators, like the TV comedian Andy Kaufman—who, twice removed, a knowing parody of a parody that doesn't know it is a parody, in some aspect of his act wants to get it across that in fact he loves Elvis, would in some part of his soul give up a limb to feel as Elvis must have felt when he sang as, in his best moments, he sang, and who, as a comedian on TV, in this context of camp layered over bad taste, cannot begin to get such a thing across. The country is aware of Elvis as he is presented in TV movies: just one more confused star, an ordinary boy with a bit of talent and a bit of nerve who lost his way. Someone we can

33

Bill Bell, front sleeve of New Age Steppers LP *The New Age Steppers* (On U, U.K.), 1981.

all easily identify with, and just as easily feel different from, safe from.

We've had scores of books in which the Elvis who first attracted our attention is unrecognizable: books full of nice memories, books full of awful tales. We're going to get more of the last: Albert Goldman's forthcoming biography—it will be published next month, there will be ads everywhere, it will be excerpted in your newspapers and reviewed in *Time* and *Newsweek*—may have enough dirt in it to bury everything else. Goldman is a vulture with no interest in his subject; he's already made hundreds of thousands of dollars from his book and he'll make more. He's got, as they say, a lot of good stories. So what if he doesn't know, or care, what he's talking about—doesn't know, that is, why the world is at such a point that a book about Elvis Presley could make so much money? What we want to know is why a certain person sang in a certain way, and why that touched us, why that simple confluence of circumstances changed the country, and the world—but since those are difficult questions, mysteries that will never be solved but also the only questions worth asking, we can be led to settle for every last quirk, rumor, failing, perversion, and we may be led to believe, finally, perhaps, that the real questions are not so important, or even real at all. A certain person, singing in a certain way—maybe it wasn't quite what it seemed. Anyway it was a long time ago.

As we form or accept the idea of Elvis that America will live with, or live without, whether it is an idea of beauty or an idea of squalor, we are moving farther and farther away from the source of that idea: Elvis Presley's music. But even the story, the life, is losing its shape; it's being reshaped to fit into old boxes. The scandal books and the loving memoirs tell the same story in the

34

end, an old story that is not, in any particular sense, Elvis's story: he got what he wanted but he lost what he had. He was cut off from his roots; he fell from grace. See what happens to American heroes; see what we do to them. We've always loved this story: the artist or the leader dies for our sins, after permitting us to enjoy them.

Such mythologizing predated Elvis's death, but it's gathered irresistible force since. A dead person is vulnerable in ways a living person is not, and it's not simply that you can't libel the dead. When the subject of a book is living, he or she can always make that book into a lie by acting in a new way. A dead person can be summed up and dismissed. And Elvis is especially vulnerable, because for much of America he has always been a freak.

Let me quote James Wolcott, a columnist for the *Village Voice*. "Elvis," he writes, "is a figure whose significance shrinks with each passing season. . . . As a musical artist he doesn't exist—he doesn't begin to exist." Wolcott is a snob but he's not a fool, and he's not an old hack with a grudge against rock 'n' roll. Wolcott is twenty-eight, and he's written well about rock 'n' roll; he was one of the first writers to spread the word about punk. But now he's most interested in making a name for himself, in attracting attention, and this is one way of doing it: such a complete dismissal of Elvis Presley has not really been heard, in an interesting publication, since the fifties.

What exactly is Wolcott saying? "As a musical artist he doesn't exist—he doesn't begin to exist"—even as simple musicology such a statement has no meaning unless we're willing to wipe out most of the history of American popular music, most of blues, country, and rock 'n' roll, from ancient Child ballads like "Barbara Allen" to the Sex Pistols' "Anarchy in the U.K." It has no meaning unless we're willing to write off that music as a bad joke, a trick we played on ourselves. Wolcott's line tells us we can forget it—but we shouldn't forget that a great proportion of the American public has always believed precisely what Wolcott wrote. With Elvis dead, we're going to hear a lot more of this: as ridicule, and as silence. 35

There are other ways in which Elvis, dead, is vulnerable, other ways in which he is being dismissed. Alice Walker is a black writer from Georgia who once wrote a great, shattering novel called *The Third Life of Grange Copeland*. She recently published a short story called "Nineteen Fifty-five." It's about a white pop singer who records a song by a blues singer, a black woman. The record makes the pop singer famous, rich, powerful. He feels guilty, though—not because he used the woman's song, though he is grateful, but because, after singing the song hundreds of times, on record, on television, all over the country, he still doesn't understand it. So he plies the woman with gifts: a car, a house. He brings her on TV to sing the song with him; he has her over to his house, hoping she'll tell him the secret. Finally he dies—alone, fat, ruined, helpless, too young—dies because he couldn't understand the music that made him a star. He couldn't solve the mystery; he couldn't even find it.

Now, there is truth in this story: the truth that, in the music Elvis sang, there is a mystery. But that was hardly the point Alice Walker was making. Her point was blunt—blunt enough that even the reviewer for the *New York Times* recognized that "Nineteen Fifty-five" was a parable about Elvis, Willie Mae Thornton, and "Hound Dog"—a song Thornton was the first to record but which, as it happens, she did not write. The story isn't, in the end, a real piece of fiction—a story that generates its own reason for being— it's an argument about the nature of American culture: about how white America was sold, and happily bought, a bill of goods, and about how black America was bilked. The white boy robs the black woman—pays her, yes, dutifully, piously, even, but some things can never be paid for—and dies of guilt.

This story has no more meaning than the statement that as a musical artist Elvis doesn't exist, but a search for meaning is not at issue here. The story is an object that will insulate those predisposed to accept it, and that will turn some readers away from music they might have otherwise heard, or that they have already heard. Never mind that part of what needs to be understood is not the mystery of Willie Mae Thornton's "Hound Dog"—a recording that is good, but ordinary, a piece of genre music—but the mystery of Elvis's "Hound Dog," which was a sound for which no one was prepared. Listen: the idea that Elvis didn't understand this song is bewildering. But if we accept that we don't have to talk about Elvis—a person who did a particular thing at a particular time, for particular reasons—then the story fits neatly into various cultural prejudices, some of which are those of American blacks, and more of which are those of white, middle-class Americans, and it makes perfect sense.

Writing about Elvis's death, rock critic Lester Bangs talked about how Elvis had given a generation a sense of itself as a generation, and how, well before Elvis died, those who had once felt that felt it no longer. "I can guarantee you one thing," he wrote: "we will never again agree on anything as we agreed on Elvis." Today it is clear that Elvis's fans, people who get some sense of life through some reflection of this person, don't speak the same language, which may tell us that they, we, never did. We have an Elvis who is dissolving in sentiment, an Elvis who has nothing to do with sex, drugs, misery, tragedy, anger, resentment, simply a perfect man. We have an Elvis dissolving in horror and crime. We have an Elvis dissolving in shared myths that existed long before he did and that will exist long after. We have an Elvis whose work is being dissolved by the facts of his life, as anyone's work can be dissolved by the facts of his or her life.

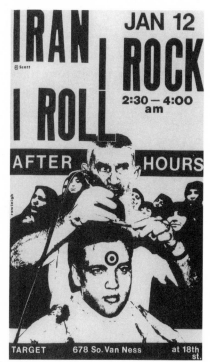

There is a way to respond to this. It's to place ourselves in confrontation with Elvis's music—all of it, pieces at a time, trying to understand what's there, what isn't, how the music was made, how it communicates, how it fails to communicate. We have to understand that not every little boy or girl can grow up to be Elvis Presley. We have to understand that if Elvis is an exemplar of the American dream, that tells something about the limits

Raleigh Pardun, "Iran I Rock I Roll," flyer for Target Video, San Francisco, 1980.

of the American dream—because Elvis was unique, talented in a way that no one else in this century was talented, as Howlin' Wolf was talented like no one else in our history in so far as we know it, neither of them missing parts of a formula, but pieces that made everything else fall into place around them.

British critic Simon Frith sheds some light on the morass that is now Elvis—on our inability to encompass the Elvis of 1968, singing "Tryin' to Get to You," and the Elvis of the bourbon bottle. "Our joyous response to music," Frith writes, "is a response not to meanings but to the making of meanings. This response involves self abandonment, as the terms we usually use to construct and hold ourselves together suddenly seem to float free. Think of Elvis Presley. In the end this is the only way we can explain his appeal: not in terms of what he 'stood for,' socially or personally, but by reference to the *grain* of his voice. Elvis Presley's music was thrilling because he dissolved the symbols that had previously put adolescence together. He celebrated—more sensually, more voluptuously than any other rock and roll singer—the act of symbol creation itself."

I disagree with Frith at the end—Elvis didn't just, or even principally, dissolve the symbols that had put adolescence together, he dissolved the symbols that had put America together. As his career went on, those symbols regained their shape, and surrounded him, trapped him, made it hard for us to see him at all, made it nearly impossible to see him as anything more than a simple symbol of all the other symbols. But the grain of his voice remained—that element in his voice that rubbed against, that rubbed raw, so much that we had taken for granted, as finished and sealed. That element told its own story: it changed, it disappeared, it reappeared, it kept on making symbols, submitting to old symbols, then casting them off. And we can still hear it happen. Today we did.

Simon Frith's words are just a beginning. The surface has only been scratched, and the surface has been covered up. It's so covered with debris we can't even see the scratches, can't feel them as we run our fingers over the old 45s.

Every once in a while, though, someone gets it right. Someone pins it down—not the answer, but the reality of the question. Someone reminds you that, no, it wasn't an illusion; it wasn't a trick. The insistence we've heard in Elvis's music that nothing is settled, that nothing is final, that there are new things under the sun, comes home. And because of the grime crusted over the records, this now happens less often, less directly, when one listens to the music than when someone else catches what is there, and finds new words for it.

William Price Fox is a North Carolina novelist who once wrote a terrific trash novel called *Ruby Red*, about two country girls who sing their way to success and perdition in Nashville; when he wrote about the way their voices intertwined, you could hear it. Earlier this year he published a novel called *Dixiana Moon*, about a young New Yorker and an old Southern hustler who join forces to stage the ultimate revival show. One night, driving through the South, the New Yorker picks up an old Sun single on the radio. "Wonder what he was like," he says to his carny mentor. "He wasn't like anyone," says the would-have-been Colonel Parker. "You start trying to compare Elvis to something and you can forget it. . . . All you can do with a talent that big and that different is sort of point at it when you see it going by, and maybe listen for the ricochet." We are the ricochet.

1979

Duets

The following memorandum was recently passed to this magazine by an anonymous source in the Consumer Complaint Department of an unnamed state. We reprint it here in the public interest.

After the appearance in *Billboard* magazine of an item implying that the 45 rpm release of "Save the Last Dance for Me," credited to Mr. Jerry Lee Lewis, was in fact a duet (circa 1961) between Lewis and Mr. Elvis Presley (lately deceased), weekly sales of over 100,000 copies were claimed by the Sun Records label (currently the property of Mr. Shelby Singleton of Nashville, Tennessee, who purchased the company from its founder, Mr. "Sam" Phillips of Memphis, in 1969). Almost immediately, this office was deluged with calls from irate consumers, many of whom insisted that the "second voice" alternating with that of Lewis "sounded no more like Elvis than my Uncle John" or, in some cases, "than my Aunt Martha." Though, according to *Billboard*, one recognized expert, Mr. "Doc" Pomus, "says he is sure it is Elvis," Pomus's testimony can perhaps be discounted, since he is the coauthor of the composition in question and presumably stands to profit from whatever notoriety it might receive.

The release of a "follow-up" long-playing record, however (*Duets*, credited to Lewis "and Friends," also on the Sun label), obviates all doubts, and gives grounds for action under Title IX. We have made these determinations:

1. Neither Elvis Presley nor, to squelch a particularly bizarre story, his twin brother Jesse Garon (officially stillborn but long

rumored to have been kept alive since 1935 for use in an "Elvis Resurrection") appears on *Duets* in any manner. The "Elvis" voice is likely that of Mr. "Jimmy" Ellis, who in 1972 recorded an imitation of Presley's "Blue Moon of Kentucky" (also released under the auspices of Mr. Singleton, and also with the implication that it was a previously unreleased recording by Presley). This performance, according to an authority on the Sun label, "fooled Sam Phillips," but we have ascertained that Phillips heard the recording only once, and then over the telephone, at four in the morning, during an especially heavy hailstorm.

2. The selection, "Am I to Be the One," previously issued on the Lewis long-player *A Taste of Country*, is an authentic duet between Lewis and Mr. "Charlie" Rich, and is not "country," but "rock 'n' roll."

3. A number of selections (notably "C. C. Rider" and "Cold Cold Heart") seem not to have been made by either Lewis or Presley, a circumstance which, if provable, mandates action under titles XXI, CLX and MXXII.

4. Lewis himself has not been of assistance in this matter. When asked who might have played on the recordings he made during his tenure at the Sun label, he replied only (as he has apparently done in the past): "*I* played on 'em! What the [expletive deleted] else do you need to know?"

Therefore, we recommend action as noted above. Furthermore, given rumors of a planned "Mystery Beatles Reunion Album," an "Elvis Meets Kate Smith Album," and a "Jam Session" featuring the late "Buddy" Holly, "Ritchie" Valens, and "The Big Bopper," we recommend that this department place an established "rock critic" on retainer.

Respectfully submitted . . .

Terry Allen, cover illustration for "Clones: The PostScript Impersonators," *Publish! Desktop Publishing*, November 1989.

1978

Tales from the Crypt

Poking around Munich shortly after the death of Elvis Presley, filmmaker Diego Cortez discovered a cache of photographs taken by one Rudolf Paulini in 1959. They showed Elvis—then in the Army and stationed in West Germany—visiting the Moulin Rouge, a Munich nightclub. Putting the Paulini pictures together with some *Stars & Stripes* shots of Elvis in uniform, plus a short text by critic Duncan Smith, Cortez had himself one more Elvis book.

But *Private Elvis* carries images of Elvis that heretofore could only be dredged up from deep dreams and scabrous fantasies. These are images of Elvis young and beautiful, still unafraid of the world he'd conquered, and yet the result is a succubus of a book, repulsive and irresistible: Elvis-porn.

The book is structured like a dream. It begins with the *Stars & Stripes* photos (Elvis with his duffle bag, on a troop train—you've seen this before), tinted a deathly, greenish black. The section ends with a hint of what's to come: Priscilla Beaulieu, just fifteen and standing with her mother, waving goodbye to Elvis as he leaves Germany at the end of his hitch. In the style of Michael Lesy's riveting detail enlargements for *Wisconsin Death Trip*, the same shot is placed on the facing page, but blown up and with Mrs. Beaulieu cropped out: suddenly, with only Priscilla to look at, we see that she is transfixed by lust.

Out of this almost official narrative, skewed just slightly, we're plunged into the Moulin Rouge. With the pages now tinted magenta, we go through the looking glass.

Elvis, dressed in civilian clothes and a complacent sneer, has   43 stumbled into a Diane Arbus retrospective. At least, that's what one sees today. In concept and execution Paulini's photographs are straight and unconceived: he snapped Elvis with waitresses, showgirls, fans, bodyguards, whores, posing, kissing, mugging. But just as Michael Lesy found hellish secrets in the prosaic work of a turn-of-the-century Wisconsin camera-for-hire, Cortez makes the work of an ordinary nightclub shutterbug, snapping patrons and then trying to get them to pony up, seem like a come-on for the slimiest orgy.

There's seediness—a tawdry, corrupt aura—to the almost 150 pages of Moulin Rouge pictures that does not mesh with the Elvis we carry in our heads, no matter who that Elvis is or how false we now know him to have been. The women we see him with are mostly grotesque: the clash of fat, of heavy, clumsy makeup, of rotting teeth and junkie faces with Elvis's smug vitality makes a silent noise. Girls flash by: they draw Elvis in, their practiced seductions changing him before our eyes from idol to pimp. When a stripper thrusts her tongue at Elvis's ready mouth you want to turn away, so you turn the page and run flat into a blowup that makes you see what you don't want to see even more clearly.

Elvis looks straight at the camera. It's as if he wants to tell us—what? That he knows, and doesn't care, that these pictures will violate every other image, from his baby photo to the *National Enquirer*'s coffin portrait? That, punk, you'll never understand? As Lewis Carroll drawing up a brief for the Red Queen, Duncan Smith doesn't make a fool of himself trying to understand:

Elvis was always aware that he had to recognize himself as a recognition on the part of others. It's not like Elvis produced any of it, he's not the author of Elvis, he is ex-centric to his own Elvishood. [My God, what a phrase.] But others could not accept the alienation effect displacing itself onto another person. Elvis knew of his own duplication, but he also knew that its transgression was impossible because he was, by Law, the original duplication. Elvis's lawyers insisted on his remaining Elvis; Elvis was only Elvis in signature, in writing, and that was required by Law.

Rudolph Paulini, Munich 1959, from Diego Cortez, *Private Elvis*, 1978.

. . .

The pictures are images of a displacement that will not be displaced: there is total distance in Elvis's face as he digs his fingers into the flesh of women who in normal times the Colonel would never have let near him, and there is also complete comfort, a sexuality that is no less disturbing for its passivity. And there's something else, a bigger story: American health in an erotic smashup with European decay.

Like Elvis's distance and his comfort, health and decay merge. You can't tell them apart. And that's what makes these pictures pornographic. You don't even need the movie they're stills for.

46

1981

The Myth Behind the Truth
Behind the Legend

MONEY

When Lamar Fike, for many years a member of the Memphis Mafia, Elvis Presley's stable of paid friends and gofers, decided to sell his story, he spawned a small industry. Agent Kevin Eggers brought Fike together with Albert Goldman, a fifty-four-year-old pop critic and former college professor. The word went out that Fike had the goods, and Goldman was to give the goods some substance—to turn what might have been just another scandal book into "the definitive biography." Serious money was put behind the project, and it paid off. Before publication, Goldman's *Elvis* generated well over $2 million in subsidiary rights: a $1 million U.S. paperback sale, a $400,000 U.K. paperback sale, a movie option, high-priced excerpts in *Rolling Stone* and *Ladies Home Journal*, newspaper syndication through the *New York Times* service. Because of the money involved, and because of Goldman's reputation as a New York intellectual, the book has been reviewed widely and prominently; as no book on Elvis Presley before it, it has been taken seriously. Despite some partially negative or carping notices, the reviewing media have accepted the book as it presents itself—as the last book we will need about Elvis Presley.

SCANDAL

The promised scandal is there in plenty, and because of the saintliness in which Elvis was wrapped throughout his lifetime, it still has punch. There is first of all dope, Herculean quantities of it; then sex, orgies, and homemade pornographic videos piled upon

47

fetishes, phobias, and neurotic dysfunction; then violence, a much thinner theme, but including accounts of cruelty, gunfever, and gunplay; then fat, then waste—all of it testimony to a schizophrenia as out of control as it was cossetted. But the significance of Goldman's book is not to be found in its collection of scandals— Lamar Fike's memories, rumors, composite scenes, old stories fleshed out or simply repeated. An exile from the real world, Elvis Presley built his own world, and within it—where the promise was that every fear, pain, doubt, and wish could be washed away with money, sex, drugs, and the bought approval of yes-men—Elvis Presley rotted. It was a fantasy of freedom with the reality of slavery, the ultimate validation of D. H. Lawrence's dictum on what he took to be the American idea of freedom: "Men are not free when they are doing just what they like. The moment you can do just what you like, there is nothing you care about doing." The real significance of Goldman's *Elvis* is in its attempt at cultural genocide.

HOW TO DO IT

It is Goldman's purpose to entirely discredit Elvis Presley, the culture that produced him, and the culture he helped create—to altogether dismiss and condemn, in other words, not just Elvis Presley, but the white working-class South from which he came, and the pop world which emerged in his wake. For such a task, revelations about the moral weakness and ill-spent life of a single individual are useful, but no matter how numerous or squalid such revelations might be, they are not sufficient. It is necessary to utterly destroy the individual's claim on our attention by leading the reader to feel in every way superior to him; to sever the individual from the social context that might make sense of his work or allow the reader to feel kinship with him; to bury what might remain of that social context in bigotry and stereotyping; to selectively omit important parts of the story being told, and to falsify others; and to surround the enterprise as a whole with calumnies and lies.

48

SO WHAT

Were it not for the money behind the book and the consciousness of the book that money has produced, Goldman's *Elvis* would be little more than a 598-page attempt to prove that Albert Goldman is better than Elvis Presley, just as Goldman's earlier *Ladies and Gentlemen, LENNY BRUCE!!* was a 555-page attempt to prove that Albert Goldman was hipper than Lenny Bruce. How else to explain Goldman's bizarre aside that because Elvis was uncircumcised, "he saw his beauty disfigured by an ugly hillbilly pecker," unless one assumes Goldman is inordinately proud of his own lack of a foreskin, and wants everyone to know about it? But because the book is having its intended impact, and because Elvis Presley is so large a figure, intertwined with the lives of millions of people in ways that have hardly begun to be examined, a good deal is at stake. What is at stake is this: any book that means to separate a people from the sources of its history and its identity, that means to make the past meaningless and the present incomprehensible, is destructive of that people's ability to know itself as a people, to determine the things it might do as a people, and to discover how and why those things might be done. This is precisely the weight of Goldman's book, and it is precisely the weight of the cultural genocide he wishes to enact.

HILLBILLIES EAT DOG FOOD WHEN THEY CAN'T GET SHIT

It is hard to know where to begin: the torrents of hate that drive this book are unrelieved. On Elvis's background: "The Presleys were not an ordinary family: they were hillbillies. . . . A more deracinated and restless race could not be imagined. . . . Just as the hillbillies had no real awareness of the present, they had no grasp on the past. . . . [Vernon and Gladys Presley were] the original Beverly Hillbillies. . . . [Gladys Presley was] not merely ignorant, but a hillbilly Cassandra. . . . [Vernon Presley was] a hard, mean, nasty redneck . . . a dullard and donkey . . . [with a] deadened dick. . . . Like most Southern men, Vernon had a

49

knack for slippin' away. . . . 'I jes' can't see mahself over theah in a fereign country' [Goldman pretending to quote Gladys Presley]." On the South: "rickets, a disease produced by not having enough money or enough brains to eat right . . . a [gospel] sing is one of those parochial institutions endemic to the South. . . . [Pentecostal Christianity] is a set of superstitions . . . the corny old saws of hillbilly faith healers . . . a classic white trash bluegrass song. . . . No matter how much of the black style these white boys take, it always comes out sounding as Caucasian as the Klan. . . . Of all the dumb activities in this dumb working-class school about the dumbest was shop: Elvis Presley's major." On Presley: "Little cracker boy . . . sang like a nigger. . . . He loved above all else to impersonate the jive-ass nigger pimp. . . . [he looked like] a homosexual in drag . . . a latent or active homosexual . . . his fat tongue . . . his mush-mouthed accent . . . his country-bumpkin cousins . . . smug, stupid, embarrassingly self-conscious screen rooster . . . [his] dumb jocko-shlocko Memphis-in-Bel-Air milieu . . . pig junkie . . . the face of a young George Wallace." On there being nothing lower than a male hillbilly like Presley except any kind of woman: "His middle-aged woman's passion for knick-knacks, curios and chatzkahs . . . throwing things like a hysterical woman . . . he would always go inside a stall, like a woman . . . like an obese go-go girl . . . propped up like a big fat woman recovering from some operation on her reproductive organs." And on, and on, and on. Right here, you have the essence of the book.

THE MYTH BEHIND THE TRUTH BEHIND THE LEGEND
"Myth," Goldman writes, "is what we believe naturally. History is what we must painfully learn and struggle to remember." Within this remarkably philistine formulation, Goldman makes much of his puncturing of Myths (his capitalization), all of which were punctured long ago, which exist to be punctured because Goldman has labored to inflate them, or which are punctured only by fiat and mystification. Goldman notes, for example, that it is a prime Presley Myth that Elvis took much of his style from free-wheeling

50

GREAT POP THINGS → THE HERB J. GOODMAN STORY

"only the names have been changed to protect the guilty !!!!" By Colin B. Morton & CHUCK DEATH

THIS EXPLAINS WHY HE NEVER GOT ANY OLDER OR ANY FATTER !!!!

BALDERDASH!

YOUR HORSE IS A BUTTERFLY MATE

FIDDLESTICKS!

POO!

Australian born Herb J. Goodman sold his thriving colonic enema parlour in London's Earl's court to finance the publication of his "ELVIS: VooDoo SEX ZOMBIE" in which he claimed that Elvis had been killed in action during the Vietnam War and revived by his manager Colonel Sanders using chicken-blood! ....

? ०००

SOUTH WAY OUT WEST Adolph Hitler BERLIN 2/2 XXX

Despite the critics constantly claiming that his horse was a butterfly Goodman went on to write "UP AGAINST THE WALL, WHITEY: the Mahatman Ghandi Story" in which he claimed that Ghandi had suggested the idea for the second World War on the back of a Christmas Card he sent to Adolph Hitler in 1938. ....

WHAT ARE YOU REBELLING AGAINST?

WHAT'VE YOU GOT?

Other little Known works by Goodman include "Nice Guys finish last: the Joe Stalin Story", "Mother Theresa, Hot Bimbo from Hell", and "Jesus Christ: REBEL WITHOUT A CAUSE" which was filmed by Russ Meyer with Dennis Hopper in the title Roll, Kitten Natividad as Mary Magdalene and Marianne Faithfull as the Virgin Mary ....

HE ONLY HIT ME ON THE NOSE....

CAVERN

TATE GALLERY

His return to the exacting science of post-contemporary biography was "SMILING ASSASSIN: the life of John Lennon" in which he postulated that Lennon was a serial-killer who had bumped several people off by hitting them on the heads with shovels. This was denied by his widow Yoko, ex-Beatle Paul McCartney and one of his alleged victims

Colin B. Morton and Chuck Death, *Great Pop Things*, "The Herb J. Goodman Story," *LA Weekly*, 25–31 January 1991.

Pentecostal preachers. One Goldman phone call, to the man who has headed the Presleys' Tupelo, Mississippi, church since 1944, confirms that services there were invariably reserved and genteel. Another Myth destroyed. There remain only a few problems. First, the minister in question arrived in Tupelo when Elvis was nine, and says nothing about services during Elvis's formative years. Second (as Goldman himself will claim when he needs to find roots for Elvis's later interest in spiritualism), the Presleys attended tent meetings and traveling revivals, where the preaching was often far wilder than in a settled church. Third, there are Elvis's own words. "The preachers cut up all over the place, jumping on the piano, moving every which way," Elvis told an interviewer in the mid-fifties. "The crowd responded to them. I guess I learned from them." Why would Elvis lie? Goldman has no need to explain, as he refrains from quoting Elvis on the point.

The real myths a reader confronts in Goldman's book are those of his invention. By far the worst of these concerns Sam Phillips, the founder of Sun Records, and the man who first recorded Presley, Jerry Lee Lewis, Carl Perkins, Charlie Rich, and Johnny Cash, and who made the first important records with Howlin' Wolf and many other blues singers.

NIGGER

Perhaps the most famous statement in the history of rock 'n' roll is that attributed to Sam Phillips by Marion Keisker, his co-manager at Sun during the early and mid-fifties, and in fact the person who truly "discovered" Elvis—noting his name, vocal style, and a phone number at which he could be reached after the eighteen-year-old showed up at the Sun studio to make a "hear-your-own-voice" record so that he could hear his own voice. The statement is simple and elegant. "If I could find a white man who had the Negro sound and the Negro feel," Keisker remembers Sam Phillips saying, "I could make a billion dollars."*

In Goldman's book what we are offered is very different. "If I could find a white boy who sang like a nigger," Goldman has Sam Phillips say, "I could make a billion dollars."

Goldman presents himself as a hipster (in fact he is a hippie, in the fifties meaning of the term: one whose only interest is to appear hipper than anyone else in the room), and perhaps to the hipster, who alone comprehends the primal genius of the black man, all non-hipster ofays are racists, but Sam Phillips was one of the great pioneers of racial decency in this century. He worked with blacks day in and day out, and in the fifties, in Memphis, he was ostracized for it: "Hey Sam," he heard, "you smell okay today—must not have been with those niggers!" Sam Phillips ran the only permanent recording facility in Memphis, and he had opened it solely to record black musicians.

Inspired by Goldman's example with the Tupelo minister, I picked up the phone and called Marion Keisker in Memphis. (Though Goldman claims to have based his book on more than six hundred interviews, neither he nor his researchers ever spoke to either Keisker or Phillips.) I read her Goldman's version of Phillips's statement. This is what she said:

"UNDER NO CIRCUMSTANCES! What? I never *heard* Sam use the

---

* From an interview with Keisker by Jerry Hopkins, as it appears in Hopkins's *Elvis* (1971). Sam Phillips denies making the statement, believing (according to Keisker) that it implies he was only interested in money, when his ambition was equally to bring the two races and their music together.

word 'nigger'—*nothing* could be more out of character." She paused to catch her breath. "Never. Never—*never.* I don't believe Sam ever used that word in his life, and he certainly never used it to me."

Thus we have the myth behind the truth behind the legend.

The effect of Goldman's revision will be twofold. Because his book will be the most widely read and widely consulted biography of Elvis Presley, his perversion of Sam Phillips's statement will replace the statement itself: it will be quoted in reviews, articles, among fans, and in other books, and it will defame the reputation of Sam Phillips.* And because Goldman has placed a racist slur at the very founding point of rock 'n' roll, and because, here and elsewhere, he works to make racism seem ordinary, matter-of-fact, and obvious, he will contribute to the acceptance of racism among rock fans, who might learn a different lesson from an honest version of their history, and he will contribute to the growing fashionableness of racism among Americans of all sorts.

DEGENERATE

If not racism, then eugenics. Having established "hillbillies" as a "deracinated race," Goldman sets out to prove that Elvis's line was the most degraded of all—resurrecting the long-discredited theories of Henry H. Goddard, who in 1912 published a study of the "Kallikak" families (from kallos, the Greek word for beauty, and kakos, for bad). According to Goddard, a "Martin Kallikak" had a one-night stand with a bar woman of low morals, and later married a Quaker. The first liaison produced a line of criminals, drunkards, and morons, while the second produced only "the

---

* One of those who followed Goldman's version was Robert Pattison, professor of English at Long Island University and author of *The Triumph of Vulgarity: Rock Music in the Mirror of Romanticism*, published in 1987 by Oxford University Press. After receiving galleys of the book, I wrote the publisher, pointing out the distortion and insisting on its seriousness. The publisher replied that the author was sure Goldman's words were correct, because they were "more vulgar," and that, in the annals of popular music, "vulgarity is always closer to the truth." Pattison was topped in 1991, in the *New Republic*, by Louis Menand. "Everyone who writes about popular music," he said, "knows that before Sam Phillips, the proprietor of Sun Records, recorded Elvis Presley in 1954, he used to go around saying, 'If I could find a white boy who sang like a nigger . . .' "

highest types of human beings." The findings thus proved that poverty and antisocial behavior (and, conversely, wealth and good character) were entirely a matter of inheritance—of genetics. The purpose of the study was to affirm that the poor were poor because they were inferior, that social programs (for, say, the eradication of pellagra—or rickets) were a waste of money, and that certain sectors of the American population had no place in society. Goddard bolstered his research—he could ascertain a person's level of imbecility by a glance or by hearsay—with faked photographs. "Goddard's Kallikak family functioned as a primal myth of the eugenics movement for several decades," Stephen J. Gould writes in *The Mismeasure of Man*. Longer than that: as late as 1961, many years after Goddard himself had repudiated the import of his work, his falsifications were presented as fact in a major American psychology textbook.

Finding "strong reason to believe" that Bob Lee Smith, Elvis's maternal grandfather, may have married a first cousin, Goldman gravely informs his readers that "genetics may explain why the children of Bob Lee's brothers and sisters turned out well, whereas Bob and [his wife] Doll produced children who exhibited an abnormally high incidence of addiction to drugs and alcohol, emotional disorders and premature death." Goldman turns his tricks well. While most of *Elvis* is written in the voice of the hipster ("they's many a crazy, likah drinkin' pill-poppin' countrah boy that kin get hissef jes' as racked-up 'n' ragged as the craziest coon on Beale Street"), in the addled syntax of a person who dictates rather than writes ("envying what is beyond one"), or in the tones of a man who simply can't be bothered with decent language when the subject of that language is so obviously contemptible ("What really bugged Elvis was that they could never find one of those trick cars, like they have in the circus"), here Goldman slips easily into the simultaneously vague and definitive cadences of the social scientist. Thus he offers the litany, familiar to anyone with a passing knowledge of the literature on eugenics, of "violence," "convulsions," drink, birth defects, and "homicidal madness," until

54

"Finally one comes to Elvis, whom we see now as possibly the victim of a fatal hereditary disposition."

Whatever that means—and of course outside of Goldman's intentions it means nothing at all. There is no such thing as "a fatal hereditary disposition." But the claim does have its purpose. Is it possible that the rot, the schizophrenia, that took over Elvis was in some way bound up in the fact that as a working-class hero who (no matter how great his fortune) never left the working class, Elvis could not integrate the worship and derision which were his fate from his twenty-first year? That Elvis's life represented a real American dilemma? By no means. It was all in the genes of the "bad side" of the Presleys, and the Presleys were part of a "deracinated race" from the start. As Goldman says, "there is absolutely no poignance in this history."

MIMIC

In order to destroy Elvis Presley as an American original, who might tell us something worth knowing about America, Goldman moves to destroy Elvis as an American ("The Presleys were not an ordinary family: they were hillbillies"), as a person ("Elvis was a pervert," we are told, because, Goldman reports, he was fixated on "the vision of black pubic hairs protruding around the edges of white panties"—a pervert, presumably, like James Joyce, who was fixated on the vision of white panties with little brown spots on their rear sides), and as an artist. Goldman has some positive things to say about a few of the early Sun recordings, though they were, he reminds the reader, nothing new (Elvis's "notion of what was hip was almost quaint"), little more than "parodies," and essentially fake: Sam Phillips "attached to his new star's raw and untrained voice the electronic prosthesis [Goldman means the slap-back echo Phillips had used earlier on many blues records and used later on many rockabilly records] that masked his vocal faults while it transformed—or shall we say transfigured?—his vocal quality into the legendary Presley sound." After a justifiable dismissal of "Heartbreak Hotel," which was less an Elvis record than

55

an attempt by RCA to bring him into the pop mainstream, Goldman mostly ignores the rest of the early RCA work and, when Elvis returns from the Army, jumps straight into a condemnation of such bloated (and still exciting) discs as "It's Now or Never," omitting any mention of *Elvis Is Back!*, the powerful blues and R&B album with which Elvis in fact announced his return to pop music. When it comes to the unrehearsed, small-combo rockabilly blues of the 1968 comeback TV special—certainly the most mature and passionate music Elvis ever made, and very likely the best music he ever made—Goldman writes it off as not even worth consideration as "a document," reserving his praise instead for the shlocky Broadway arrangements that made the rest of the show so conventional. He must do this because the small-combo music can be credited to no one but Elvis himself, who not only sang but played lead guitar—and Goldman grants approval to Elvis's music only when it can be credited to someone else.

To make a rejection of Elvis's music credible, though, Goldman must discredit both the response that greeted it (easily done: "broad, coarse effects . . . appropriate to all the broad, coarse sensibilities in his audience . . . [rock] was little more than a gag reflex regurgitating the high school enthusiasms of the Swing Age") and the possibility that it had authentic roots. Having already disposed of the Myth that Elvis absorbed, and transformed—integrated into his personal culture—the spirit of unfettered Pentecostalism, Goldman turns to the great question: "How did Elvis learn to sing black?"

Forget that Elvis's first records were rejected by white DJs as too bluesy and by black DJs as too country—forget that to people who knew Southern music, Elvis's version sounded new. To Goldman, Elvis was simply an inspired "mimic": he learned what he knew off the radio. His music had no human source, which is why it was not real music—it was just another commodity, and it was learned as a commodity.

Which leaves, for Goldman, one more Myth to be taken down: the Myth that Elvis spent time on Memphis's Beale Street, drawn there by the blues. Goldman wastes little space on the problem:

"all one has to do to test that idea is to imagine how Gladys would react to such a pastime. Why, every weekend people got killed down on Beale. No, it is unthinkable that the boy who spent his weekends listening to records at Charlie's would slip into the darkest and most dangerous part of the ghetto to hear somebody sing the blues."

Robert Henry and Nat D. Williams are two more Memphians who somehow missed being interviewed by Goldman. Henry was a Beale Street promoter. "I taken him to the Hotel Improvement Club with me," he told Margaret McKee and Fred Chisenall, authors of *Beale Black & Blue*, "and he would watch the colored singers, understand me, and then he got to doing it the same way as them. He got that shaking, that wiggle, from Charlie Burse, Ukelele Ike we called him, right there at the Gray Mule on Beale.* Elvis, he wasn't doing nothing but what the colored people had been doing for the last hundred years. But people . . . people went wild over him."

Nat D. Williams, the unofficial mayor of Beale Street, was also a history teacher, a newspaper columnist, a disc jockey, and emcee at the Palace Amateur Nights on Beale Street. He described Elvis's performances on those occasions to McKee and Chisnell: "We had a lot of fun with him. Elvis Presley on Beale Street when he first started out was a favorite man. When they saw him coming out, the audience always gave him as much recognition as they gave any musician—black. He had a way of singing the blues that was distinctive. He could sing 'em not necessarily like a Negro, but he didn't sing 'em altogether like a typical white musician. He had something in between that made the blues sort of different. . . . Always he had that certain humanness about him that Negroes like to put in their songs. So when he had a show down there at the Palace, everybody got ready for something good. Yeah. They were crazy about Presley."

Henry and Williams are recounting events that took place well

---

* Sam Phillips recorded Burse's "Shorty the Barber" in 1950—Burse was only the second artist to record for Phillips—but did not release it.

before Elvis showed his face at Sun Records, and well before an electronic prosthesis was grafted onto his voice. Black people apparently did not notice the absence. And while *Beale Black & Blue* was published only recently, the information it contains has been available for years in Memphis to anyone willing to ask for it—as has the information that Elvis, whatever his mother might have thought, spent time as a teenager in Memphis's black neighborhoods, having sex with black girls. Such information is missing in Goldman's book not because it is dubious, but because it conflicts with Goldman's portrait of Elvis as "an unregenerate Southern redneck who stopped just short of the Klan."

IN HIS PLACE

And that, I think, is enough. I have little stomach for any more: for an accounting of Goldman's countless factual errors (Hank Williams's death dated in the wrong year; "James Meredith," who has surely suffered enough, being killed in 1969 at Altamont rather than Meredith Hunter), misspelled names, songs placed in the wrong movies, or the dismissal of James Brown as "an African witch doctor" and of Roy Brown, the voice behind B. B. King, Bobby "Blue" Bland, Elvis Presley, Clyde McPhatter, and Jackie Wilson, as a "mediocre bluesman." One can pause and say that Goldman has done useful work elaborating the truth about Colonel Parker (though he is not the first to reveal that Parker is a Dutchman rather than the West Virginia carny Parker has always made himself out to be), and about Parker's long-term mismanagement of Elvis's career; one can say that the opening chapters of the book, set late in Elvis's career behind the walls of Graceland and inside the Hilton International Hotel in Las Vegas, while clearly composites, are effectively creepy. One could detail the homophobic, ethnic, and racist slurs, the exaggerations, and the undocumentable assertions and conversations that mar even these sections of the book. But there is no point.

"The fascination," Linda Ray Pratt has written of Elvis, "was the reality showing through the illusion—the illusion of wealth and the psyche of poverty; the illusion of success and the pinch of ridicule; the illusion of invincibility and the tragedy of frailty; the illusion of complete control and the reality of inner chaos. . . . Elvis had all the freedom the world can offer and could escape nothing." It is that pinch of ridicule—the ridicule in which a great part of America has always held Elvis Presley—that is the exploitative basis of Goldman's book. Even the book's errors, its disregard for the most easily confirmed facts, its degraded style, and its refusal of documentation or, most of the time, even attribution, is part of this: it emphasizes that a figure such as Elvis Presley does not deserve a serious biography.

But while Goldman's *Elvis* is not a serious biography, it is a very serious book, if only for what it seeks to accomplish: to exclude Elvis Presley, and the culture of the white working-class South, and the people of that culture, and the culture of rock 'n' roll, and the people of that culture, from any serious consideration of American culture. The bait is being taken: in the *New York Times* review that will be syndicated all over the country, Christopher Lehmann-Haupt wrote that after reading Goldman's book "one feels revolted by American culture for permitting itself to be exemplified by the career of Elvis Presley."

There is no need to feel revolted: American culture has never permitted itself to be exemplified by Elvis Presley, and it never will. But certain Americans—and of course people from all over the world—have recognized themselves, and selves they would not have otherwise known, in Elvis Presley: Americans whose culture had taken shape long before Elvis Presley appeared, and those whose culture would have had no shape, would have been in no way theirs, had Elvis Presley been willing to keep to the place allotted to him.

He wasn't willing to keep to his place, and now he is being returned to it. It is altogether fitting and proper that this be so, because as a redneck, as a hillbilly, as a white boy who sang like a nigger, Elvis Presley was never permitted to join the culture that has never permitted itself to be exemplified by what he made of it.

1980

The Road Away from Graceland

Peter Guralnick has sometimes asked a question few others have ever asked: who would Elvis Presley be, how would we hear his music, if we had never heard of him? If his first Tennessee singles were someday rediscovered, as the 78s of forgotten Mississippi bluesmen of the 1920s and 1930s were rediscovered in the 1960s, if that handful of tunes could now be heard as a whole world, complete and finished, one shout, unsurrounded by the arguments of the hundreds of records that were to come? Guralnick's *Lost Highway: Journeys & Arrivals of American Musicians* is a kind of answer.

Named for one of Hank Williams's most indelible songs—a song that inspired Bob Dylan's "Like a Rolling Stone"—*Lost Highway* combines interviews, reporting, reflection, scholarship, and singing prose to render portraits of twenty vital but often ignored performers. These are men who, by means of dedication—a dedication, Guralnick argues, to their own, hard-won sense of self—have claimed places in the traditions they inherited: performers such as country singer Ernest Tubb, Memphis R&B eccentric Rufus Thomas, soul singer Bobby "Blue" Bland, rockabilly kings and outsiders Charlie Feathers, Charlie Rich, and Elvis, black singer-songwriter Stoney Edwards, bluesmen Howlin' Wolf and Big Joe Turner. To close the book there is an interview with Sam Phillips, and it is a revelation.

"You've got to understand what the prospect of meeting Sam Phillips meant to me," Guralnick writes. "Some kids dream of curing cancer, some of growing up to be President. As for me I dreamt of playing in the major leagues, winning the Nobel Prize for literature, becoming Elvis Presley's adviser and chief confidant, and—as I grew older and only slightly more realistic—meeting Sam Phillips."

From the time we first discovered Sun Records, my friends and I had constructed elaborate fantasies not just about Elvis but about the man who had [first] recorded Elvis, Jerry Lee Lewis, Carl Perkins, and before that the great Memphis bluesmen . . . who were just as much our heroes. As I got to know Charlie Rich, and other Sun artists . . . the way in which they spoke about Sam Phillips—his astonishing persuasive powers and force of mind—the way in which they recalled his ability to inspire, even as they complained about royalty rates and the eventual necessity for their leaving Sun, only fueled my vision of this behind-the-scenes Machiavellian genius who had discovered so many of the best talents of a generation.

No matter how much Guralnick brought to his meeting with Sam Phillips—in 1979, a decade out of the record business and running a new Memphis radio station (WWEE—later renamed WLVS), Phillips "had the look of an Old Testament prophet in tennis sneakers, his long hair and long reddish beard only matching the oracular tone and language that came out in the cadences of a southern preacher"—against all odds, Guralnick came away with more.

I realized as he talked that he was speaking to every fantasy I had ever had about him, that he was telling the story of how one man, and one group, had made history. . . . "My mission," he said, "was to bring out of a person what was in him, to recognize that individual's unique quality and then to find the key to unlock it." As I listened, I heard from him what my friends and I had so carefully constructed for ourselves, and I had a glimmer for the first time in a long time of the unlikely notion that history is not necessarily an accident, that the self-willed individual can affect his environment, and his times, in ways that we cannot even calculate.

But Sam Phillips—as if he sensed his words would end a book about the struggles of men to make themselves heard in public when their origins promised they would be lucky to make a private living—had much more to say.

My greatest contribution, I think, was to open up an area of freedom within the artist himself, to help him express what *he* believed his message to be. Talking about egos—these people unfortunately did not *have* an ego. They had a desire—but at the same time to deal with a person who had dreamed, and dreamed, and dreamed, and looked, heard, felt, to deal with them again under conditions where they were so afraid of being denied again

—one theme of *Lost Highway*, never stated, simply appearing, is the effort some of its subjects make to hide the fact that they cannot read—

it took a pure instinctive quality on the part of any person that got the revealing aspects out of these people. It took an 'umble spirit, I don't care whether it was me or someone else. Because I knew this—to curse these people or just to give the air of, "Man, I'm better than you," I'm wasting my time trying to record these people, to get out of them what's truly in them. I *knew* this.

Like Phillips's legacy—Elvis's "Mystery Train," Lewis's "Whole Lotta Shakin' Goin' On," Perkins's "Blue Suede Shoes," Howlin' Wolf's "How Many More Years," so many more—Guralnick's book is almost too rich to take in at once. The intensity and empathy of his portraits is so great I could not read *Lost Highway* straight through: I would finish a few chapters, put the book aside, and then helplessly muse over Ernest Tubb, patiently signing LPs for men and women who had followed his music for forty years, over Stoney Edwards's will to make songs out of circumstances that might have killed other people, about the patent madness of Charlie Feathers, after twenty-five years still crying out of oblivion that it was he, *he* who taught Elvis everything Elvis ever knew.

For all of its riches, though, *Lost Highway* traces only one road—strangely, as if the superhighways of fame and money are really only backroads to the truth. "I never wanted to be a critic" is Guralnick's first sentence, and while he fights against giving in to his own voice—the last words of his chapters are almost always those of their subjects, and Guralnick's analysis is rarely direct, but rather piggy-backed onto narrative—he nevertheless insists on a very specific critical vision, rooted in a very specific set of values. And I think it is a narrow vision.

The best writing about American popular music—like the best popular American music itself—reveals hidden but profound connections between styles, performers, communities, races, and historical periods that at first glance seem all but self-contained. While this is always true of *Lost Highway*, the book is defined by a more subtle argument: that if artists cannot and should not be separated from each other because one plays blues and another country, they can and should be separated from each other in terms of how they choose to act out their commitment to their music, and on the basis of how deep that commitment may be judged to be. For all its stylistic groupings, *Lost Highway* is less a study of musical genres, or even of individual performers, than a very closely observed and broadly applied study of vocation: an attempt to define the most valid form of music as work, and as cultural politics.

To Guralnick, such work and politics—politics as the attempt to identify a community, even to call it into being, and then to say what that community is and what it might best do—take place somewhere outside the mainstream, in the gap between success and failure. Here, shadowed by the past, an artist's work and politics have more to do with finding and keeping a voice than with confronting change in the world through changes in one's art. Both work and politics find their source, then, in small, rural, religious communities—even if, as a professional entertainer, the

63

artist has moved away from his beginnings, and is now a sinner who lives in the city.

The performers who figure in this book, black and white, sing music "from the heart," music that is deeply engraved in their background and experience. All make reference to this . . . all recall a boyhood in the country, on the farm, a shared experience that links them inextricably not to the undifferentiated mass audience that television courts, but to a particular, sharply delineated group of men and women who grew up in circumstances probably very much like their own, who respond to the music not just as entertainment but as a vital part of their lives.

The values that power such a social fact are honesty, sincerity, refusal of ambiguity, loyalty between performer and audience, stoicism, endurance, and dignity—the antithesis of pop trash, sensationalism, irony, persona, frivolousness, or outrage. One performs to bind people (or *a* people) together, and to confirm their identity—not, as in the most vital pop moments, to divide people and thus to force them to question who they really are. Though in the world of Guralnick's performers the pursuit of success is an economic and often psychological necessity, it is not a source of inspiration: it "seriously, inevitably distorts the very core" of the performer's "being, as well as the music itself."

At sixty-three, Ernest Tubb is something like a mirror image of [his] fans. Although his hair is still dark and he continues to hold himself erect in his turquoise suit, white Stetson, and gleaming brown boots, the once-lean frame has filled out, and the bags under the eyes, wattles under the chin, and slow crinkling smile all give him the look of the plain hard-working men and women who come out to see him. It is almost as if, having cheated fate once when he escaped the bleak West Texas farmland on which he was raised, he has only met it in another guise further on down the line, as his origins make themselves plain in the worn weathered features, the honest creased roadmap of his face.

64

This is a passage of surpassing harmony. One reads it and thinks, "This is how it ought to be." It is a perfect summation of Guralnick's point of view, and it confirms Guralnick's fundamental conviction: "entertaining people on a mass level is no longer genuinely popular culture . . . but a pathetic dilution of a rich cultural tradition."

All of which is, to me, deeply appealing and not at all satisfying. I like minority culture, outsider culture that refuses to compromise with the mainstream—but there is no greater aesthetic thrill than to see minority culture aggressively and triumphantly transform itself into mass culture, suddenly affecting the lives of millions of people who were not prepared for it, and then to see that minority culture face a test it itself was not prepared for, to see if it can stand up against the bargain mainstream culture is always ready to make. And that is what happened when, twenty-five years ago, a host of minority cultures—blues and country, bands of escaped tenant farmers white and black—came together and, stealing what they wanted from the mainstream, from Swing era jazz and bland white pop, from big-city noise and suburban materialism, re-formed as rock 'n' roll. Though in the mid-fifties Memphis music often called back to the past, or to a present that was already dead—on one of his Sun singles, Carl Perkins sang about taking his girl out for a date on a horse—the city was emerging from long years of domination by Boss Crump, finally feeling the pull of the postwar boom, and unsettled by the migration of thousands of Deep South farmworkers, like Elvis's parents, who had seen the advertisements they believed the rest of the country were already living out. The town was less a home for folk culture than for a bohemia: a secret culture within the commercial culture every Memphian took for granted. ". . . this [was] like Paris at the turn of the century," Memphis musician James Dickinson once said. "We saw a change in Memphis that affected the whole world." Centered around Sam Phillips's Sun studio—soon to be known as "the chicken-shack with the Cadillacs out back," a place of private languages and coded gestures, of talismans and disguises, pink   65 and black, a secret public—it was a milieu in which unknown tongues were spoken and unmade things were made to happen, and also, as Donovan once put it, a launching pad for "beatniks out to make it rich." The mainstream absorbs, it breaks down, it spits out, it buries and it destroys—and it is also changed.

Guralnick's vision of good culture leads him away from hard questions about why some artists fail to reach the audiences their music seems to deserve, and about why some artists fail to develop as artists. It also leaves out too much—too much that Guralnick himself values—and makes too much inexplicable. What do we make of an expatriate like Van Morrison? How do we understand Bruce Springsteen, who refers less to a marginal community of shared experience than to a mass community governed by a shared mythology? Chuck Berry's music—that unique but instantly right, instantly recognized hybrid of blues, country, Frank Sinatra, hipster humor, and ads for the 1955 Coupe de Ville—was not made for "a sharply delineated group of men and women who grew up in circumstances" like Berry's own: just the opposite. Rather than drawing on a minority culture that resisted the homogenizing embraces of the mainstream, this outsider sought to join the mainstream, to become its prophet and its critic. The pursuit of success did not "distort" Berry's music; it virtually created it.

Such an achievement does not make sense within Guralnick's framework—and neither, at bottom, does the achievement of Elvis Presley. The fire in his Sun singles would never have been there had his gaze not been fixed on horizons far beyond those almost everyone around him took as absolute borders; for that matter, those singles would likely have never been made if Sam Phillips hadn't heard, somewhere, a billion dollars in Elvis's voice. Listen to the rehearsal version of the B-side of Elvis's very first single, an old Bill Monroe bluegrass tune, and Phillips's joy at the end of it: "Fine, *fine*, man, hell, that's different! That's a *pop song now*, little guy!"

Joni Mabe, *Elvis Tours Central America, Brings Hope to Hopeless, Food to the Hungry,*
1984.

1984

A View of Graceland:
The Absence of Elvis

In 1957, Elvis Presley, at twenty-two the most famous man in America (save for President Eisenhower and General Douglas MacArthur, who had won their glory in other times, and with whom Elvis Presley was in only metaphysical competition), bought Graceland, a 1939 white-columned mansion in Memphis, Tennessee. With his mother (until her death in 1958), his father, his grandmother, various cousins, his payroll of friends and hangers-on, his teenage ward who became his wife, his daughter, and finally his girlfriend ("Fiancée!" she insisted, too late), he lived there until his death in an upstairs bathroom on 16 August 1977. Depending on how you saw it, he had been either a ludicrous white-trash fraud or the greatest artist in American history. In the years since his death, one hears in Memphis, more people have visited his grave on the grounds of Graceland (catching a glimpse of his mother's storied pink Cadillac in an open carport) than have visited the grave of President John F. Kennedy. Graceland itself was closed to the public until 1982, when its first floor was opened for tours; in 1983 Graceland Enterprises, Inc., hired William Eggleston to take official photographs.

What one first sees through Eggleston's eyes is no kind of house, but a 1957–77 version of King Tut's tomb. Unlike the walls and furnishings in Walker Evans's 1936 photos of an Alabama tenant farmer's shack, photos of which Eggleston's are inevitable descendants, these walls and furnishings cannot speak. The silence is overwhelming. There are no echoes of the assiduously contrived

68

amusements or the long hours of boredom that took place here. It is impossible to believe that anyone ever lived in this place.

One can look in vain for revelation. Elvis Presley's secrets, hidden from himself perhaps more than from his audience, were in his music; his house is an attempt to say that none were ever necessary. FLORET PAUPER could have been chiseled over its entryway, saying all that the house ever meant to say.

The first shock an Elvis fan experiences upon visiting Graceland is that the mansion is only barely set back from the road (today, Elvis Presley Boulevard): that through its gates one can see, as Elvis Presley saw, a shopping center, every shop in which now sells only Elvis Presley souvenirs. Boiled down to postcards, Eggleston's images belong in those shops far more than in his art gallery.

Which is to say that while the Graceland visitor will not see what Eggleston saw, he or she deserves to. Born and now living in Memphis, but raised in Mississippi (reversing "Born in Mississippi / Raised up in Tennessee," the Delta blues motto that described postwar Southern migration, and which Elvis lived out), Eggleston is a sophisticate with a New York agent, no Elvis fan but an outsider with a cool gaze; across his twenty-five or so photos one can follow his careful path through the Graceland labyrinth, through generations of poverty and humiliation, a moment of conquest, and millions of dollars (or tens of thousands of dollars), all of it incorporated into a living room, a bathroom, a television room, a music room, a Taking Care of Business room. But one feels less like a visitor than an intruder. In the early fifties, I lived in a middle-class suburb of San Francisco; a block from our cozy street was an open field with a rotting farmhouse, rented by a large family with strange accents, the Stackhouses. We called them the Shackhouses, of course; at school the children dressed shabbily and no one played with them. After a developer bought the field and evicted the family, my friends and I broke into the abandoned wreck, marveling at the containers of flours and coffee—brands we'd never seen on our own mothers' shelves—dumping the contents on the floor, at once thrilled and shamed by our privileged burglary.

These are the feelings provoked by Eggleston's best photographs. There are ordinary shots in his portfolio, shots of the graveside Meditation Garden or of fans' graffiti on the stone walls on the street side of the house, arty versions of thousands of wire service photographs of the same things. The lucid pictures are of the rooms, their walls raised in the compositions as if by an architect, their furnishings placed as if by a decorator, in neither case by whoever those people were, but by Eggleston.

Two skewed corner shots, of a room holding a television (the color scheme is white and gold) and another an organ (the color scheme is indescribable: the ceiling is quilted, the walls are covered with drapes that effect an effete version of quilting, on the drapery is a framed assembly-line pastel of a generic European city), are the most silent, because both rooms were established to produce sound. One doesn't credit that they ever did, and not because the rooms are museum-pristine: the carpet in the TV room is scuffed, the paint on the door jamb in the organ room is flaking off. Rather the rooms seem still in readiness for the arrival of he whom they were meant to please. Eggleston's overbright color presses the sensation: the pictures look like 1950s painted photographs. You see a house that was built, that was decorated, but that was never inhabited.

Never inhabited by whom? By the corporeal Elvis, films of the autopsy on the body of which, it is said, can be had for a price? By the "Hound Dog" Elvis, the rocker, which, its fans must believe, could never have been contained by such squalid gentility? By the once indigent, always ridiculed Elvis, the boyhood deprivations of which have been prettified from the first press releases to the present-day birthplace shrine in Tupelo, Mississippi—the Elvis for which no mansion could ever be more than an inverted reminder of a legacy that could never be escaped? Those long hours of boredom, when Elvis's retainers waited downstairs for him to awake, perform his toilet, and then descend, and who then waited for him to announce what it was he wished to do or, failing that, to offer suggestions of their own ("Hey, El! Wanna fly this model airplane in the *house?*"), are finally in those pictures—a deco bar, a room draped in blue framing a gold piano, a room with a break-front on top of which a white marble bust of a Greek god looks out over a speckled white marble bust, mounted on a black-streaked white marble coffee table, of Elvis Presley—not as presence but as absence.

I haven't visited the inside of Graceland, just the grounds. But all those I know who have been inside—people who to a real degree shared Elvis Presley's class background, and whose lives were formed by his music—have returned with one word to describe what they saw: "Tacky." Tacky, garish, tasteless—words others translate as white trash. There is not a hint of this in Eggleston's photographs. In the end what they communicate is an irreducible dignity, and though the pictures could not be less naturalistic, less objective, though one can't tell if this is Eggleston's contribution or simply what he found, that intimation of dignity populates the house, despite the insistent absence of the man who bought the house and lived in it.

Looking, it becomes clear that Walker Evans's pictures of a 1936 tenant farmer's shack were as unnaturalistic and nonobjective as Eggleston's pictures are of Graceland. This is mildly interesting, if one is interested in aesthetics—but it is worth remembering that in 1936 Elvis Presley lived in a similar shack; that at that time Walker Evans took many photographs in Tupelo, Mississippi; and that Elvis Presley, twenty years later the most famous man in America, might be known to us today, had things turned out differently, only as a nameless face in a famous Walker Evans photograph. Just as Eggleston's photos are inevitable and contrived descendants of Walker Evans's photos, Graceland was an inevitable and contrived descendant of the shack Walker Evans pictured; the transition is powerful as art because it did not work as life.

Charles Burns, cartoon for cover of *Greed* #4, 1988.

The Return of
Elvis Presley

1985

The Last Breakfast

Over the past month, avoiding Elvis Presley—you remember him—required some fancy footwork. January 8 marked his would-have-been fiftieth birthday; all stops were pulled. There was *A Golden Celebration*, a six-LP boxed set of mostly unreleased recordings; eight conventional reissues; an into-the-future MTV video for the rerelease of "Blue Suede Shoes"; *Elvis: One Night with You* on HBO, fifty-two uncut minutes of marching-through-Georgia jam sessions originally taped for the 1968 comeback special; a tour of Graceland on Showtime, hosted by Priscilla Presley; features on every network news program; an all-Elvis *Entertainment Tonight* at double the show's normal length. Plus a tribute from the president, recycling his Bruce Springsteen endorsement-in-reverse from last year's campaign: "America's future rests in a thousand dreams inside your hearts. It rests in the message of hope in songs of a man so many young Americans admire: Mississippi's own Elvis Presley. And helping you make those dreams come true is what this job of mine . . ." Well, no. Not exactly. Stop me before I kill more. But it wouldn't have seemed out of place. You get the idea.

A Golden Celebration—outtakes from the 1954–55 Sun sessions, the complete soundtrack to the 1956–57 TV appearances, searing concerts recorded in 1956 in Tupelo, a side of the '68 improvisations, much more—is full of surprises. In Tupelo, at the Mississippi-Alabama Fair and Dairy Show, where eleven years before a ten-year-old Elvis Presley had won second prize for his version of "Old Shep," the crowd is tearing itself to pieces; people

74

are being trampled. Elvis tries to calm the audience with a brief address on the difference between art as act and art as representation. "Here's a song that says you can do anything," he says, introducing "Blue Suede Shoes." "But don't. Just don't." No luck: riot is the only proper response to what Elvis and his combo have already done with "I Got a Woman." The year before, in Memphis, still no more than a local noise, he'd been in the studio, trying to catch the soul in "When It Rains, It Really Pours," a number first cut by Sun R&B singer Billy "The Kid" Emerson. There are a couple of lazy false starts; then the twenty-year-old rolls into the tune with so much lust it sounds as if he's singing naked.

It's fabulous stuff—and, in the present moment, somewhat beside the point. The active aesthetic fact today is not that Elvis Presley once lived, but that he is now dead. The point is closer to what, in the present moment, takes place at 7:35 A.M. each weekday on San Francisco's KFOG-FM.

"It's time . . . for 'Breakfast with Elvis,' " announces disc jockey M. Dung. You're thrown back by a torrent of Elvis's hugely operatic *WELLLLLLLL*s; then there's a quick splice to "Shake, Rattle & Roll" ("Well, roll my breakfast, 'cause I'm a hungry man"), or perhaps to *Elvis Sails*, an interview EP recorded on 22 September 1958, the day PFC Presley left the U.S.A. for Germany (Newsman: "How long has it been since you've had a chance to eat today?" Elvis, sounding depressed: "Well, I ate breakfast . . ."). Then another interview, Elvis full of confidence, a good beat in his speech: "Rock 'n' roll music, if you like it, if you feel it"—Dung interrupts with an echo so dank he seems to be speaking from Elvis's stomach: "Feel it, *feel it*"—"you can't help but move to it"—which falls smack into the kinetic opening notes of the first guitar break in "Hound Dog," even though one now understands, through the magic of aural collage, that "movement" here means bowel movement, not toe-tapping. Dung "opens the doors" to the "KFOG kitchens" (sounds of pots clanging, cafeteria line forming), and the day's "celebrity chef," a listener phoning in, offers the menu Dung has promised to cook for the King, who is described as waiting patiently, but anxiously, almost desperately, for his first

75

meal of the day. And this is Elvis not as he revealed himself in 1954, or 1956, or 1968, but as he dropped dead on 16 August 1977: a glutton bloated beyond memory.

The menus began, in the fall of 1984, straightforwardly enough. Then they went regional (Tennessee catfish and grits, Maryland soft-shell crabs dripped in milk batter, a spread catered by Brennan's of New Orleans), ethnic (Italian, Polish, Chinese; for Rosh Hashana, kosher), organic ("He's been looking a little puffy lately," said the day's caller). Then they took off.

First came a junk food blitz climaxing with Moon Pies garnished with Snickers bars. Then petit déjeuner à la Zippy the Pinhead: linguine sprinkled with crushed Alka-Seltzer, an oatmeal omelette dressed with Liquid Paper, and waffles spread with Vaseline, all washed down with a bottle of Pagan Pink wine. "I just got to work at the pet hospital," a woman said the next day, "and I was feeding the dogs, and one of them was a real *hound dog*, if you know what I mean, and of course it reminded me of the King, and, ah, the food looked pretty good, and so, for Elvis's breakfast today: Kal Kan liver and beef, a side of Kibbles, and a nice bowl of water. Chow down, Elvis."

"I held a seance in my living room last night," said a man the following morning. "We made contact with Elvis, and he can't believe what you've been feeding him. His stomach is going haywire. He wants something *normal*. You're going to make him scrambled eggs, three pieces of toast—two buttered, one with butter and a touch of strawberry preserves—orange juice, and coffee. And that's *it*."

Earlier, one Peter Wood had mailed in his menu on cassette. Mustering a fine middle-period Elvis ballad voice, and accompanying himself on guitar to the tune of "Heartbreak Hotel," Wood sang:

> Last night while I was dreamin'
> I heard somebody scream
> And there was Elvis, baby, lookin'

Hungry and mean
He said, Well, I'm so hungry, baby
Yeah, I'm so hungry, baby,
I feel so hungry, I could die

Well, I fixed him up a breakfast
Of poached eggs and ham
A toasted English muffin, covered with
Strawberry jam
But he just looked at me
And then he cried
I been so hungry, since I died

So I went to the kitchen
And left the cupboards bare
Fixed him up a breakfast that was
Beyond compare
Well, French toast and omelettes, baby
Green beans and ham hocks, baby
He ate so much, I thought he'd die

Well, buttered baked potatoes
I fried him up hash browns
I made him little pork sausages that
Were freshly ground
Hot gravy biscuits
Cheese dip on Triscuits
He said, I've had enough

Given the backdrop of scandal lowered ever since Elvis ceased
to take regular meals, it has to be emphasized that from beginning
to end "Breakfast with Elvis" is made in a spirit of love—gleeful,
even vengeful love, but love nonetheless—and so have the countless
similar manifestations of the last seven years. Together they have
formed a great common art project, the work of scores of people
operating independently of each other, linked only by their de-

termination to solve the same problem: who was he, and why do I still care?

It began, perhaps, on legal terms: Elvis's death liberated those who wished to confront him from the strictures of libel and commercial exploitation.* The opening shot was perhaps Diego Cortez's 1978 *Private Elvis*, his collaged collection of photos showing a nice American Army boy sticking his tongue down the throats of Munich whores; it was outstripped by "Elvis Drugs," a fantasy commercial from Michael Nesmith's 1981 video *Elephant Parts*. Nesmith opened on a fresh-faced preteen girl in pigtails; in the background were three or four adults draped over couches and chairs, stoned out of their minds. A thick, hearty, doo-wopping Elvis voice came up on the soundtrack, remaining constant. Girl:

Hi! Are your parents forgetting to take their drugs?
Mine used to, too.
Now that they're getting older, they do forget.
But the truth is, now is when they need them most of all. Running the world is a bitch, and they were *totally unprepared for it*.
So what can you do to make sure they get off every day?
Give them these [holds up handful of pills in the shape of guitars and shoes]: colorful, pleasant-tasting *Elvis Drugs!*
They make drug-taking fun! Parents love 'em! They remind them of someone who shaped their *early moral judgments!*

Elvis Drugs!
All Shook Uppers—
Love Me Tenderizers—
Blue Suede 'ludes!
Elvis Drugs!
The fun way for adults to get the drugs they need!

---

* From the mid-1980s on, federal court decisions and new laws passed in Tennessee and California—in every case, partly as a result of suits and complaints brought by the Presley estate—abolished the common-law presumption that "the dead have no rights," and established the right of heirs to proprietorship over the "image" of a dead person, "image" being defined as a particular and recognizable attribute, be that name, face, gesture, or manner. "The lines 'round my eyes are protected by a copyright law," as Mick Jagger put it on *Aftermath*—in 1966.

Scores of bathetic Nashville tribute singles were released in the month following Elvis's death (most remarkable was Billy Joe Burnette's "Welcome Home Elvis," sung in the voice of Jesse Garon: "El, I been waitin' forty-two years. . . . Not long ago, Mama joined me here. . . . She's waitin' for ya, Elvis. Yeah, she's right over there. And soon our daddy will take our hand, and we'll be a happy family once again"). But since then punk performers have told the story, from X's brutal "Back 2 the Base" (a crazed soldier on a city bus screams curses at Presley's corpse while terrified passengers try not to notice) to the Butthole Surfers' "The Revenge of Anus Parsley" to the Nightingales' inspired "Elvis, the Last Ten Days" (over a thin staccato beat, a thinner voice chants "previously unreleased diary entries": "Day 6—Why do I feel guilty? I'm not to blame. . . . Day 10—I'm too tired to do anything today. But tomorrow I'll start my diet, and answer some of my fan mail"). In the same mode were William Eggleston's creepy Graceland photographs, Tony Fitzpatrick's voodoo pastel *The King Poisoned by Spiders*, Donigan Cumming's exhibitions of photos of praying Elvis fans orchestrated by tapes playing their testimony, Joni Mabe's huge, found-objects installation *I Wanted to Have Elvis' Baby, But Jesus Said It Was a Sin* ("She sees Jesus and Elvis as being similar," an interviewer reported. "Both are worshipped, are 'very passionate,' and emanate a 'sense of helplessness' "), the telephone-pole punk flyers made from and turning into the same found objects, cartoonist Gary Panter's pursuit of Elvis zombies loose in Japan, and Eddie Murphy's parodies, predictable as stand-up comedy (in the middle of "My Way," Elvis farts), anything but as ensemble television. One *Saturday Night Live* skit opened in a gas station outside Memphis, with a grease monkey and his guitar-thumping pal discussing reincarnation, and whether a few Elvis items might not pump up their business; they decide that if the King came back he'd be offended. Just then two women, draped in Elvis souvenirs, on their way home from Graceland, rush in shouting: they've run over someone, they need help. Together the four drag back an unconscious Eddie Murphy, a local in Levi's. As he revives, he begins to talk like Elvis, half-singing

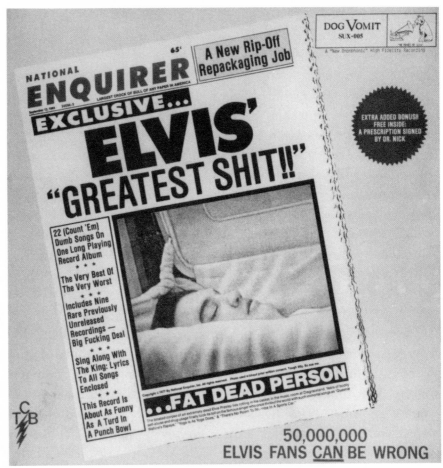

Front and back sleeves of bootleg LP *Elvis' "Greatest Shit!!"* (Dog Vomit), 1984.

"Can't Help Falling in Love"; he asks where he is, who he is. "You're—the King!" says the astonished guitar player. Murphy—there's less of him all the time—flounders; he doesn't understand. "What's my name?" he says. Guitarist: "Elvis . . . Aron . . . Presley!" Murphy: " 'Elvis Presley'? That's a *name?*" The guitarist strums a few chords, and Murphy chimes in automatically, first on "Love Me Tender," then "Jailhouse Rock," then "That's All Right," sounding more like Elvis with every note. Suddenly, he gets it; it all comes back. The Hillbilly Cat whips a comb out of his back pocket, cocks a hip, and struts toward a mirror . . .

Overreaching even that was *Elvis' "Greatest Shit!!"*, a bootleg LP on the Dog Vomit label comprising nineteen of Elvis's most abysmal movie tunes, plus a few bonus tracks. The cover pictured Elvis in his coffin, captioned "FAT DEAD PERSON . . . Years of bodily self-abuse and drug usage finally took its toll on the famous singer who once thrilled the world with such immortal songs as 'Queenie Wahine's Papaya,' 'Yoga Is as Yoga Does,' & 'There's No Room to Rhumba in a Sports Car.'" Inside the sleeve was a reproduction of the prescription made out to Elvis by Dr. George Nichopolous on 15 August 1977: "Dilaudid, 50, Quaalude, 150, Percodan, 100

. . .'' The album was perversely listenable. "But why's this on it?" said a friend, as side one closed with "Can't Help Falling in Love." "That's not 'shit.' " Then, on this unquestionably authentic out-take of one of Elvis's loveliest ballads, he lost the beat. "Aw, *shiiiiiiiiit*," he said.

All of these things, and a hundred more like them, converge on the reversal of perspective that has been punk's contribution to contemporary culture: a loathing that goes beyond cynicism into pleasure, a change of bad into good and good into bad, the tapping of a strain in modernist culture set forth by avant-garde artists from de Sade to George Grosz to Céline. Punk turned that strain into ordinary culture, ordinary humor, which is to say ordinary life. It provided the context that makes *Elvis' "Greatest Shit!!"* listenable and "Breakfast with Elvis" a work of everyday art.

The people who call in to KFOG are not punks; KFOG is not a punk station. But the emergence of punk simultaneously with the death of the founding rock 'n' roll saint ("Good riddance," said Johnny Rotten) was pure serendipity. On formal punk terms, Elvis's status as a corpse legitimized him—made him an interesting subject, a fecund metaphor. In the amorphous, wholly unformal domain of pop culture at large, Elvis's death made him human: a man who walked and talked, tripped, stumbled, and fell, and babbled like an idiot. Floating in the air, an incipient conflict if only on the level of a son or daughter's ugly new haircut, punk added the frisson that brought the newly human Elvis back to life.

Throughout his forty-two years, Elvis Presley was made to stand for decency: good manners and clean living. Following his death, consciously or not, his fans and inheritors—those who had loved his music, and those who, like Johnny Rotten, merely knew that had Elvis never been born they would have never entered public life—felt betrayed. They felt betrayed even if, like Johnny Rotten, they believed that decency was a bourgeois scam ensuring only that without power and money you'd get your blue suede shoes stepped on the minute you walked out your door. Elvis was a sinner: he was a hypocrite.

Yet Elvis's sins sparked a sense not only of betrayal but of confirmation—"Celia shits!" as Jonathan Swift put it. Making bad good, punk was able to turn hypocrisy upside down. Elvis's tawdry death sanctioned that of Sid Vicious, and when Vicious went out with "My Way"—for which, by the end, Elvis had exchanged "Can't Help Falling in Love" as the last word of every tawdry concert—his death sanctioned Elvis's. Together, they freed their fans to indulge themselves. For the first time, it was possible to really play with Elvis Presley—to give voice to every fantasy.

In 1982, at the fourth annual Salute to Memphis Music, in a seminar attended by working-class, Christian Elvis fans (all women, save a foreign student), I listened to a no-holds-barred debate over whether or not Elvis Presley had gone to heaven. Punk has fixed on the same question. In the fanzine *Flipside*, one comes across a Raymond Pettibone cartoon showing a young decedent in white gown and angel's wings, tears streaming down his face: "You're just faking! Elvis is here; we know it. Tell us where he is! Show us Elvis!" A neosurrealist magazine arrives in the mail with a picture of Elvis in bat wings printed on the mailer. "All dressed up like an Elvis from hell," runs a line from a Gun Club song: it's an image that calls up Jim Jones of the People's Temple, who so clearly modeled himself on the post-comeback, black-helmeted Presley. "Money Fall Out the Sky," by Cool It Reba, a New York post-punk band, is about pop success; after covering the financial side of the issue, the singer gets down to cases:

> I want to live—like Elvis
> Drive a car—like Elvis
> I wanna sleep—like Elvis
> Walk around—like Elvis
> Take drugs—like Elvis
> Make love—like Elvis
> Go to hell—like Elvis

In Memphis in 1982, the women who took up the question of whether Elvis went to heaven weren't sure of the answer; neither is punk. "Rock 'n' roll," Elvis says on the *One Night with You* special, "is basically gospel music—well, it sprang from that . . ." True or false, it's inarguable that rock 'n' roll inevitably drags whoever wants to talk about it to religious metaphors: "Forgive them, they know not what they do," the Showmen sang of antirock zealots in their 1961 hit "It Will Stand." It is no coincidence that, in the beginning, Elvis was damned as an antichrist, and that after his death he was celebrated by Sam Phillips, a serious man, as an avatar of the Second Coming, just as it is no coincidence that Johnny Rotten, turning the strain that carried Grosz and Céline to himself, announced himself with the words "I am an antichrist," and then posed nailed to a cross.

So there he is: begging for food on KFOG, burned down in "Back 2 the Base" ("Elvis sucked doggie dicks!" shouts the soldier), drawling "Aw, *shiiiiiiiiit*." Had he reached his allotted threescore and ten, he would have remained what punk rhetoric forced Johnny Rotten to say he was: an old fart, a bore. Instead he died at the right time: death and punk have kept him working, and given him a new measure of freedom, as they have his fans. No longer does any fan have to feel small—except in those odd moments, "I Got a Woman" delivered from the stage in Tupelo in 1956, or "When It Rains, It Really Pours" on *A Golden Celebration*, when the ineffable says hello.

Punk didn't change the world, but like all pop explosions it changed the way some walk through the world, the way some talk about it. Punk revealed the contingency of every social fact; its enemy was always hegemony, the self-presentation of domination as nature. By the time of his death, Elvis himself had become hegemonic—not because he had traduced President Richard Nixon into making him an honorary narcotics agent, but because the seeming invulnerability of his performance, and its emptiness, had made his music seem fated, an objective and merely historical fact; in Memphis in 1954 and '55, it had been a subjective choice. Today he says what he was never permitted to say in either moment; he says what he never permitted himself to say. I'm hungry, he says. I want. I don't care—gimme.

84

"You know what you did to make me love you," he sang in 1955, halfway through "When It Rains, It Really Rains." "You really opened up my nose." Memphis writer Stanley Booth was listening with me; he had followed Elvis from the beginning, had seen him take the stage in Memphis in 1956 and promise that "them people in New York and Hollywood are not gone change me none." Booth's mouth dropped open. " 'My *nose*'?" he said, grinning. "No wonder they had to wait until he died to put that out."

JULY 11—JULY 29

OUTSIDE
THE CLOCK:

BEYOND GOOD AND ELVIS

CURATED BY ROBERT LONGO

SCOTT HANSON
G A L L E R Y

415 West Broadway, New York, NY 10012 Phone: 212/334/0041 Fax: 212/334/0963

Scott Hanson Gallery, advertisement for exhibition, *Artforum*, Summer 1989.

1978–1991

Never Bet the Devil Your Head Gallery

LIFE IN
HELL

KIDS WANT to KNOW

IF YOU EAT A WHOLE BOX OF FIZZIES, THEN DRINK A GLASS OF WATER, WILL YOU EXPLODE?

WHY DO BABOONS GOT SUCH BIG RED BUTTS?

CAN DOGS SMELL FEAR?

WHY DO THEY CALL THEM URINAL "CAKES"?

IF YOU PUT A PENNY ON THE RAILROAD TRACK, WILL IT MAKE THE TRAIN DERAIL?

IF YOU DROP A PENNY OFF T TOP OF THE EMPIRE STATE BUILDING, WOULD IT KILL SOMEBODY?

IF EVERYONE IN MY FAMILY WAS KILLED IN A BIG AUTO ACCIDENT EXCEPT ME, WOULD THEY LET ME KEEP THE HOUSE?

HOW COME SATURDAY-MORNING CARTOONS ARE SO CRUMMY?

IF GOD IS GOOD, WHY DOES HE LET LITTLE KITTIES GET RUN OVER BY GARBAGE TRUCKS?

WHAT DOES HUMAN FLESH TASTE LIKE?

DO GERMS HAVE GERMS?

HOW COME THEY C LAKE TITICACA

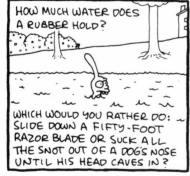

HOW MUCH WATER DOES A RUBBER HOLD?

WHICH WOULD YOU RATHER DO: SLIDE DOWN A FIFTY-FOOT RAZOR BLADE OR SUCK ALL THE SNOT OUT OF A DOG'S NOSE UNTIL HIS HEAD CAVES IN?

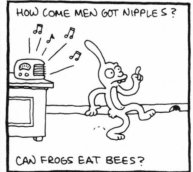

HOW COME MEN GOT NIPPLES?

CAN FROGS EAT BEES?

DID ELVIS GO TO HEAVEN OR TO HELL?

WHAT REALLY HAPP WHEN WE DIE?

Matt Groening, *Life in Hell*, "Kids Want to Know," *LA Reader*, 25 January 1985.

Richard Carseil, front sleeve of Bomb LP *From Elvis . . . In Hell* (Bogadigga/World), 1987.

Stephen Ronan, postcard, 1987.

Judith Bell, hoodoo bottle art, detail from back sleeve of Gun Club LP *The Fire of Love* (Ruby), 1981.

                    MISHIMA
          No, none at all.

He points to a FAN MAGAZINE REPORTER, directing the
press conference as he would a film.

                    FAN MAG REPORTER
                        (rapid fire)
          Your favorite writer?

                    MISHIMA
          Thomas Mann.

                    FAN MAG REPORTER
          Your most unique habit?

                    MISHIMA
          Laughing for no reason.

                    FAN MAG REPORTER
          Who would you like to be?

                    MISHIMA
          Elvis Presley.

Having gotten his laugh, Mishima redirects the questioning
to a SERIOUS REPORTER:

                    SERIOUS REPORTER
          Does this mean you'll stop writing
          novels?

                    MISHIMA
                        (grins)
          Sorry, I can't help you out on
          that one. I couldn't survive
          if I didn't continue writing one
          more line, one more line, one
          more line, one more line...

All the reporters are laughing now.

Scene from *Mishima*, screenplay by Paul Schrader and Leonard Schrader, directed by
Paul Schrader, 1985.

Jeff Leedy, front sleeve of Elvis Hitler LP *Disgraceland* (Wang Head—songs include "Berlin to Memphis" and "Elvis Ripoff Theme"), 1987.

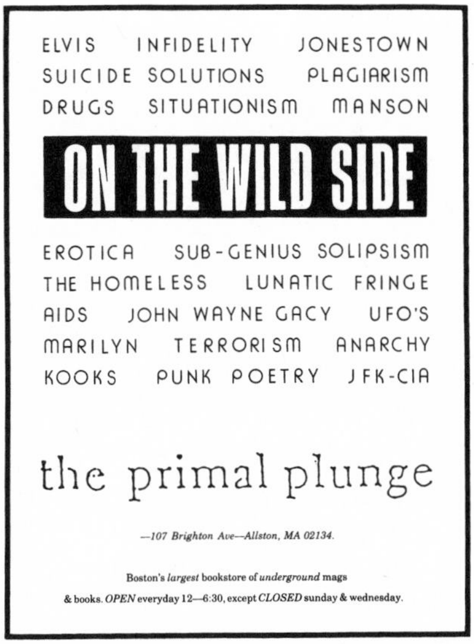

Advertisement for Primal Plunge bookstore, 1989.

The PostScript Clones Gallery: the Good, the Bad, and the Ugly

Here are the pleasant, and not-so-pleasant, visual surprises the current crop of PostScript clones produced during our printing tests. To their credit, most clones printed clean, sharp type, but occasionally, unexplainable glitches occurred.

> With the advent of desktop laser printers, designers can now generate their own greeking, saving them a lot of time and money.

> Type shops, meanwhile, have lost a minor source of easy income. After all, setting greeking is about the easiest job a type shop ever gets.

The RIPS and Princeton Publishing Labs' boards couldn't decide whether to print this text in Galliard Roman or Bold, and compromised with a mixture of both. (RIPS claims this problem will be fixed by the time you read this.) ▦

Blackout: The Eiconscript and the Lasersmith PS-415 clones darkened what should have been a gray-shaded box in Ventura Publisher. ▦

> With the advent of desktop laser printers, designers can now generate their own greeking, saving them a lot of time and money.

Macfontware without hints

> With the advent of desktop laser printers, designers can now generate their own greeking, saving them a lot of time and money.

Macfontware with hints

At press time, La Cie's Panther PDX (as well as the Abaton, Jasmine, and Qume printers) couldn't work with the hints built into Bitstream's Macfontware fonts, producing the heavy type on the left. The much cleaner type shown on the right was printed with a preproduction version of a printer controller upgrade, due out by the time you read this. ▦

---

erjet's own Printer Command Language (PCL) before printing a page.

The board's Pagemaker time wasn't as bad, but still slower than most clones and the Jetscript. In any case, the Postcard Plus made a mess of the 8-page newsletter, splattering patches of garbage graphics across a number of headlines. It also didn't print an Encapsulated PostScript page, which we tested along with our Pagemaker and Ventura documents. Abaton couldn't provide solutions for these problems.

PS-388
(board)
★★★

RIPS IMAGE 4000
(board)
★★★

The RIPS Image 4000 and Princeton Publishing Labs' PS-388 (actually a remarketed RIPS board) are the only clones we reviewed that don't act like clones—that is, they print Adobe-encrypted fonts that looked as clean and smooth as a printer equipped with Adobe PostScript would.

Besides this access to Adobe-licensed font libraries, both boards sport a RISC (Reduced Instruction Set Computer) processor that supposedly speeds printing on your Laserjet Series II beyond the speed of Adobe PostScript, although we found that wasn't the case. For example, the RIPS and PS-388 printed the long Ventura document faster than all but one of the

94

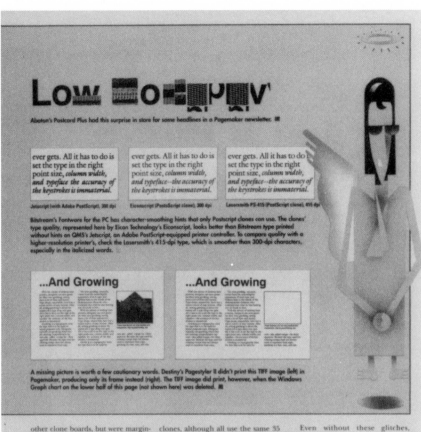

Terry Allen, angel and devil illustrations for "Clones: The PostScript Impersonators,"
Publish! Desktop Publishing, November 1989.

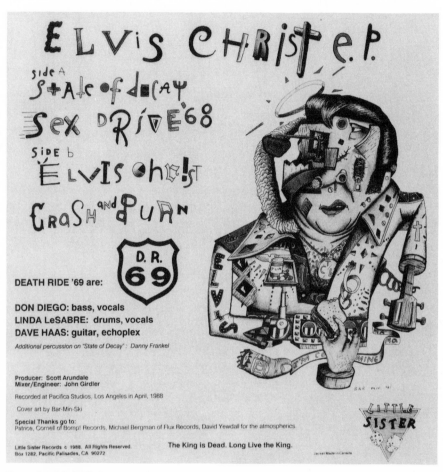

Bar-min-ski (Bill Barminski), back sleeve of Death Ride '69 EP *Elvis Christ* (Little Sister), 1988.

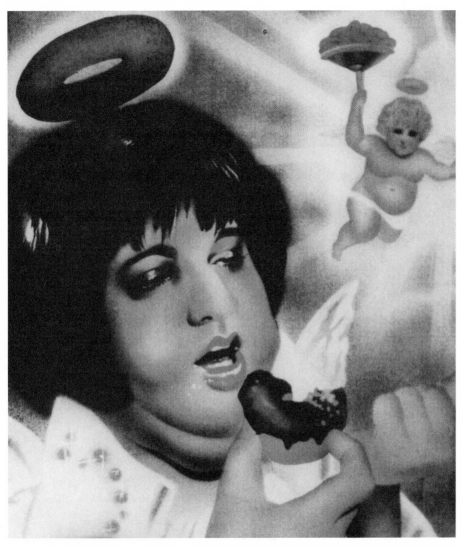

Eiko Ishioka, concept and art direction, Peter Sato, illustration, detail from *Rivals: Elvis Presley and Maria Callas, Rival Weightwatchers*, 1978.

Bill Barminski, panels from *Tex Hitler 6—Fascist Gun in the West* (Bar-min-ski Comix), 1984–85.

Torch gallery, advertisement for exhibition,
Artforum, March 1991.

1981

The King of Rhythm & Blues

Elvis Presley began as "The King of Western Bop," but what did it mean for him to become the King of Rock 'n' Roll? Joseph C. Smith's *The Day the Music Died* is a roman à clef about the music business from the time of Presley's emergence to the arrival of the Beatles. It is the bitterest book ever written about how rock 'n' roll came to be and what it turned into; its theme is racism. And its background is almost as interesting as its story.

In the early 1950s, Los Angeles had perhaps the most vital rhythm and blues scene in the country. Though segregation was hardly unknown (one could ask Mayor Tom Bradley, then a cop on a segregated police force), there was a looser racial climate than in New York, Chicago, or Cincinnati, and for every token Negro admitted to the lower rungs of white hierarchies, there was an ofay looking for another culture, and finding it. In the music business, the mix of black and white was especially creative. There were small black-owned labels that scored national hits (Dootsie Williams's Dootone, with the Penguins' 1954 "Earth Angel," was the most prominent). There were numerous integrated groups, from harmony combos like the Jaguars to Ritchie Valens's first band. The milieu was ruled by Johnny Otis, from the late forties both the top bandleader and the man you didn't cross—and he was a dark-skinned Greek-American passing for black. There were scores of lesser lights: black booking agents for white singers (one handled Ricky Nelson), white disc jockeys on black stations (not vice versa), an unstable mix of song-pluggers, producers, and songwriters. In 1952, Jerry Leiber and Mike Stoller, Jewish boys from the East Coast, were living in a leftist, interracial, male-and-female Los Angeles commune ("Marxist-Lockheed," Stoller once described the group's tendency, as the activists supported themselves working for the new aerospace company); it was at that time the future Svengalis of the Coasters wrote "Hound Dog" for blues singer Willie Mae Thornton.

Los Angeles R&B was streetwise: tunes about trouble with the law were more characteristic than such aching doo-wop love songs as the Medallions' "The Letter" ("Let me whisper, sweet words of dismortality, and discuss the pompitus of love. Put it together, and what do you have? Matrimony! Oh, my darling . . ."). In fact the legal jeopardy disc was a staple of the music—most notable were the Robins' (later the Coasters) "Riot in Cell Block No. 9" and "Framed" (both written and produced by Leiber and Stoller), and Richard Berry's "The Big Break," an outrageous follow-up to "Riot," but there were many more, including Sonny Knight's "But Officer," a 1953 non-hit that appeared on the seminal L.A. R&B label Aladdin. Three years later Knight tried again with "Jail Bird," on the tiny Vita label; he took the record to Art Laboe, a white DJ later responsible for the *Oldies But Goodies* LP series. Laboe began playing both "Jail Bird" and its flipside, a lovely ballad called "Confidential." It was the flip that took off—and after the disc was picked up by Dot, a white-owned Tennessee label known for its predatory imitations of rock 'n' roll (Pat Boone was its big star), "Confidential" broke the R&B Top Ten and the pop chart top twenty. Knight went on to back Sam Cooke and other artists; he surfaced again in 1964 with the stunning "If You Want This Love," and then disappeared. Sonny Knight was the stage name of Joseph C. Smith, who has now returned to damn the years he witnessed.

The Day the Music Died moves back and forth between four cities and four stories. In Hollywood, an idealistic young white man named Mark Donovan heads the Champ label, a subsidiary of the giant IRT complex (one can read Groove, the R&B outlet for RCA); he wants to make good rhythm and blues without ripping anyone off. In Nashville, a canny white hustler named Carl

101

Clinger starts Carousel (Dot), and amasses a fortune in country pop and pop R&B until the payola scandals force him to sell out to a conglomerate (Gulf + Western). In Chicago, an idealistic young black man named Monroe Wilcox secures the backing of a sympathetic black crime boss and forms Big City (Vee-Jay), which soon becomes the most powerful black record company in the nation. In New York, a callow white fraud named Paulie Schultz (Phil Spector) steals everything that isn't nailed down, beginning with Monroe Wilcox's first hit artists. These are pulp premises; within them Smith works with real force, drawing a picture of the relationship between art, laissez-faire capitalism, and racketeering far more vivid and detailed than can be found anywhere else.

There is cool, tough writing ("He spent three years seeing all the action a man could put up with and not drown himself from pissing in his pants," Smith says of Carl Clinger's war); there are keenly crafted stories, particularly the intricate and dramatic account of the way Monroe Wilcox turns the tables on Paulie Schultz, effectively stealing back his own group. But what really interests Smith is how a rich version of American black culture is transformed into a horrible, enormously profitable white parody of itself: as white labels sign black artists only to ensure their oblivion and keep those blacks they can't control penned up in the ghetto of the black charts; as white America, faced with something good, responds with a poison that will ultimately ruin even honest men like Smith's Wilcox and Mark Donovan.

This is a great story, and Smith opens hard. In 1956, Monroe Wilcox explains the music business to the gangster whose help he needs:

I got something [the white man] wants, bad. My music. . . . I'm going to give him as little as I can and make as much money off him as I can. I ain't gonna give it to him, or sell it to him cheap so he'll pat me on the head and tell me what a nice little nigger I am. . . . Now, I know the motherfucker is gonna throw everything at me he can, to keep me from making it. But he needs me a hell of a lot more than I need him, at least right now. . . . He's got to come to me, to get my knowledge. So I ain't going to him for a goddamned thing. I'm gonna cut my own records. Put them out on my own label. I'm gonna publish all my own tunes. Control my own artists. I ain't gonna deal with nothing personally but the colored market. . . . If I get big enough, I'm even gonna set up some colored distributors. And if I'm gonna do all that, I'll need some big money, some grand-theft money.

Smith moves from here. We see, and believe, Carl Clinger and the men who run IRT purposefully and carefully institute a new racism in the record business—a racism that, unlike the simple prewar exclusionary policies, can at once allow them to absorb, coopt, and fend off blacks without allowing them power. We see, and believe less, the market perfectly manipulated to replace artists with fakes. We see, and believe even less than that, a mob takeover of Monroe Wilcox's label. We see, and do not believe at all, that the mob has controlled IRT all along. We see, finally, that all the threads of Smith's story have been woven into a single, gigantic conspiracy.

There is no question that much of what Smith describes took place. Black artists have been systematically victimized by racism; black (and white) record companies have been taken over by the Mafia; white no-talents (though not Phil Spector, who was no no-talent) have gained riches plundering, and destroying, black culture. But little of this happened neatly, and none of it according to a precise and irresistible master plan. Given the realities of American racism and corporate capitalism, none was necessary; given the realities of American cultural miscegenation and the holes in the capitalist marketplace, no victory could be so complete.

Driven by its bitterness, Smith's story runs away from itself. The bitterness is so patently real it gives an irrational credibility to the book, but only up to a point. Once Smith begins rewriting the facts his story is based on to give his message a power the messy facts withhold, the truth in his novel—the historical truth, the cultural truth, the emotional truth—loses its own power.

As with the Don McLean record from which *The Day the Music*   103

Died takes its title, the day is here progressive, repeated, less an event than a process—but as the book nears its end, something like the day itself looms up. It's the greatest scam of all: Brian Epstein receives $750,000 from "the world's third largest body of money" to launch the Beatles in the U.S.A. Monroe Wilcox tells his gangster backer that the Mob has offered $2 million for Big City Records, because Big City holds American rights to the Beatles—who, the Mob has presumably learned from its contacts with the world's third largest body of money, are going to be the hottest thing since the Second World War.

As opposed to the rest of white rock, which he rather wonderfully calls "sewing machine music," Wilcox likes the Beatles; he thinks he may have finally found the "King" he needs to seal his control of what, at bottom, remains rhythm and blues, which means he believes he has finally found an entrée into the white market. His partner is quick to disabuse him of his hopeful notions. This is going to be worth two, three hundred million dollars to somebody, right? Maybe, Wilcox says. Well, says the gangster,

if you had $300 million, you could forget about them little white boys from England, 'cause you would be the King. Now, you know the white man ain't going for that. He may let you be the Prince for a little while, but he ain't never gonna let you be the goddamn King!

The man is right—but the game is fixed in more ways than this one. The Vee-Jay label did release the first American Beatle record ("Please Please Me," in the spring of 1963; it missed the charts), though it had nothing like exclusive rights to the group; more importantly, Beatle seed money (from Capitol, their primary label, not from Lloyd's of London or the Royal Family) amounted to only $50,000, and even that was not forthcoming until American Beatlemania was well underway, as a combination of cross-Atlantic contagion and small-scale laissez-faire hustle. It was a complex and open story, but it cannot be so in *The Day the Music Died*—to Smith, no such story could ever account for the enormity of the events that followed. There is no room in his world for anything but the curse of rock: some are born corrupt, some achieve corruption, and some have corruption thrust upon them.

Smith ultimately ends up very close to the self-serving men who promoted the payola scandals: like them, he sees rock 'n' roll as a cabal by means of which gullible consumers were victims of a sort of mind control, induced to buy records they neither needed nor desired. The difference is that Smith believes that in the best of all possible worlds white kids would have bought rhythm and blues, while the prosecutors and racist moralists behind the payola investigations thought white kids would have bought Perry Como. Neither assumption is accurate: the true racism of American pop is more a matter of audience than industry, but that is a reality Smith never sees. Closing his book as it ends in the mid-sixties, one is left on the verge of all that came next—as if nothing did.

One day in 1953, Jerry Leiber and Mike Stoller rushed back to their Marxist-Lockheed commune with big news. Willie Mae Thornton's "Hound Dog" had topped the charts. They had their first number one R&B hit. Their comrades replied with a lecture. Pop music had no social value; commercial success only proved the masses were victims of a commodity fetish and that Leiber and Stoller were its unwitting purveyors, and thus they were expelled. Had the two rock founders-to-be remained in their group after this sad incident, we would have been denied "Searchin'," "Poison Ivy," "Run Red Run," "There Goes My Baby," and "Jailhouse Rock"; had Joseph C. Smith ever joined, we would never have heard "If You Want This Love."

Mike Stoller, Elvis Presley, Jerry Leiber, at the MGM Studios in Culver City, California, Spring 1957. Photo courtesy Michael Ochs Archives.

1986

Good Book on Elvis Published— Shocking Truth Revealed

Elaine Dundy is a novelist and biographer who has accomplished a feat recent publishing history would lead one to believe is impossible: without having met Elvis Presley, or claiming any kind of fraternal or family relation to him, she has produced a book that tells you something you didn't know before. Always holding Elvis's mother, Gladys Presley, at its center, *Elvis and Gladys* is full of moments of novelty—pieces of a story that were there all along, waiting for a writer with the eyes to find them.

One of the most incisive of those moments comes early on, when Dundy goes back one hundred and fifty or two hundred years to quote a Yankee writer named James Hall on a Scots-Irish frontiersman. He could not have been much different from Elvis's early ancestors, especially on Gladys's side, Dundy argues: people who settled throughout the South in the eighteenth century. James Hall:

I thought I could see in that man, one of the progenitors of an unconquerable race; his face presented the traces of a spirit quick to resent— he had the will to dare, and the power to execute; there was a something in his look which bespoke a disdain of control, and an absence of constraint in all his movements indicating an habitual independence of thought and action.

Those words wouldn't have been out of place in 1941, when W. J. Cash published *The Mind of the South*—the type, if the frontiersman was a type, was still in place in Elvis's time. But while one can recognize Elvis Presley in these remarkable lines, they don't describe him so much as they hint at his complexity, at the contradictions that made him who he was. Along with the absence of constraint in Elvis's movements—the quality that, more than any other, shocked the world in 1956—there were the infinite constraints out of which he built his adult life; quick to resent, he was even quicker to bury his resentment. Still, two phrases are irreducibly right, as irreducible as the momentum he put into "Good Rockin' Tonight" or the easy charm of "Don't Be Cruel": "he had the will to dare, and the power to execute." The reflections of faculties that strong, that tense, shoot out inevitably to extremes: to crazed fantasies and fastidious cover-ups. And so it is with all that today surrounds Dundy's work: the bland leading the weird.

Leading the bland is Priscilla Beaulieu Presley's *Elvis and Me*. That a memoir by the woman who was married to Elvis Presley—who was, as his teenage girlfriend, his wife, or the mother of his daughter attached to him from 1959 to the day of his death—can be certifiably less interesting than any of the bodyguard/buddy books may say a great deal about the nature of the relationship, and thus about Elvis, or it may simply say a great deal about the exigencies of the cover-up. The copyright in the name of Graceland Enterprises, Inc. (which, as trustee for daughter Lisa Marie, Priscilla Presley controls), reminds the reader of *Elvis and Me* that the book has to function first and last as a Graceland souvenir.

Notable for big margins and widely spaced lines of type, the 320 pages of *Elvis and Me* take about an hour and a half to read—"which seems to have been," said a friend who read excerpts in *People*, "about the length of their sex life." Their "consummated" sex life, as Priscilla puts it—before she married Elvis, in 1967, she had, from the age of fourteen, progressively made out with, slept in the same bed with, and played dress-up video sex games with him, but there was no actual intercourse; once she became pregnant (more or less on her wedding night), there was virtually none after. But one knows all of this from Albert Goldman's biography, which trumpeted pillow-talk gleaned from Priscilla's onetime lover Mike Stone. What can *Elvis and Me* tell us that we don't know?

Not much. Something: the book leads off with the cat-scratch info that when Elvis died he was about to break up with live-in girlfriend Ginger Alden, who has since told anyone who would listen that Elvis was about to marry her. Not satisfied? All right, here's Priscilla recalling her senior year in high school in Memphis, as Elvis's Graceland "ward": "While my classmates were deciding which college to attend, I was deciding which gun to wear with what sequined dress."

It's the liveliest sentence in the book. For once and once only, Priscilla lets loose a sense of humor, touched with rage. Otherwise: "I'm a little concerned that there are too many songs in it," Elvis is made to say of the movie *G.I. Blues*, "but I think it'll work out. It had better, or I'll have a few choice words to say"—as soon as I get back from my elocution lessons. Can anyone imagine Elvis Presley speaking those lines? *Elvis and Me* offers the occasional spot of trouble (when teenage Priscilla first arrives for a visit to Graceland, Elvis doses her with enough Placydils to keep her out for forty-eight hours), and enough whitewash to cover Tom Sawyer's fence: "That was Elvis—always caring, always sensitive to everyone's needs, even while presenting a macho image to his fans."

Elaine Dundy's book is marked by the passion Priscilla left out of hers. Leaving aside Dundy's insistence that the key to Elvis's private self and public persona was Freddy Freeman, aka Captain Marvel, Jr., fave comic book rave of the young Presley, her thesis is straightforward. Elvis Presley was a creature of will, ambition, and fantasy, and those qualities can be traced to Gladys Presley. She passed them on to him—or passed them down.

It's with the passed-them-down—the genetic inheritance of character traits—that this otherwise revelatory study grinds its gears. Dundy establishes that, on Gladys's side, Elvis's great-great-great-grandmother Morning Dove White Mansell (1800–1835) was a Cherokee, and makes a case that his great-great-grandmother Nancy Tackett, again on Gladys's side, was a Jew. Interesting—fascinating. But not this:

Genetically speaking, what produced Elvis was quite a mixture. At the beginning, to French Norman blood was added Scots-Irish blood. And when you add to these the Indian strain supplying the mystery and the Jewish strain supplying spectacular showmanship, and overlay all this with his circumstances, social conditioning, and religious upbringing—especially his Southern poor white, First Assembly of God upbringing—you have the enigma that was Elvis.

What you have is a passage so ludicrous its stupidity outweighs its racism—and it's bizarre that Dundy can be so mindlessly conclusive when her step-by-step account of Elvis's forebears is so open. For that matter, Dundy silently proves such nonsense unnecessary: Elvis's physiological inheritance from Gladys was so strong it provides a field of psychological speculation irresistible on its own terms. Among the photos in *Elvis and Gladys* is a portrait of Ann Mansell Smith, Gladys's father's mother, that is a shocking match for a ten-year-old Elvis; looking in the mirror, Elvis could have imagined himself the spawn of a single genotype, the son not of his father and mother, but of his mother alone.

Dundy's sense of discovery can be infectious; it can also spin out of control. She spends much time on the long-suppressed 1937 check forgery incident that sent Elvis's father, Vernon, to prison for nine months; her suspicion that Colonel Tom Parker used knowledge of the crime to blackmail all three Presleys into lifelong submission is intriguing, but her suggestion that Parker contrived the 1957 film *Jailhouse Rock* as a sadistic practical joke, in which the son would be made to walk in his father's shackled footsteps, is worthy of the most inventive students of the assassination of John F. Kennedy. It's fun—but like Dundy's adventures in the gene pool, its only result is to make a reader doubt what truths she has to tell, and she has plenty of those.

Dundy is sensitive to the way a dirt-poor family can be shattered by the market; the Great Depression of the 1930s is part of her story, and so is the almost forgotten Great Depression of the 1890s.

The polygamy and polyandry of Elvis's ancestors makes sense in the context of economic anarchy she builds; so does their religion, or lack of it. There is never a hint of condescension. Dundy revels in a young Gladys's delight in buckdancing, and she understands why a smart, eager twenty-three-year-old woman married a near-illiterate, lazy teenager—Vernon was gorgeous. The Presleys went hungry, both before and long after Elvis was born; *Elvis and Gladys* isn't *Les Misérables*, your stomach may not knot in sympathy, but this enormously important fact means more in Dundy's hands than it has in those of anyone else. She notes that Elvis gained more than twenty pounds in his first year as a performer; the conclusion is inescapable that it was Elvis's first chance to eat.

Dundy's main project is to rescue Gladys Presley from her usual dismissal as a dumb, sentimental woman who throughout Elvis's formative years drowned him in oceans of overprotection, thus fatally retarding his emotional development and ensuring he would never grow up. *Elvis and Gladys* is a convincing argument that Elvis's infantile adult life had far more to do with class: with what, in words that can never be repeated too often, Linda Ray Pratt called Elvis's "illusion of wealth and the psyche of poverty; the illusion of success and the pinch of ridicule." Dundy quotes a letter she received from a former Memphian, who insisted upon anonymity:

I have only one overall impression about Mr. Presley's position and acceptance in Memphis. And that is naturally from the point of view of the world I was born and raised in, the world of the country club, etc. He was referred to by them as an embarrassment to the community, as his art was vulgar and common, tacky and lower class.

As the years passed and Presley's wealth as well as his fame began to benefit the Memphis charities, a transition occurred. He became known as "a fine young man." Of course, he was still secretly mocked as being tasteless and vulgar—all those many-colored Cadillacs, etc. And in the typical fashion of the hypocrisy of people of that class and its culture, or should I say lack of culture, Presley was admired but you really wouldn't want him to marry "our daughters" or sit down at "our table," or belong to "our club." But it would be nice to have him present at some social event to add some "kickiness" to the occasion. Or some fund-raising event where he would be valuable. . . .

I suspect that in a classic and tragic sense he yearned to be accepted and became a self-destructive recluse when he realized he wasn't. Perhaps he would have been accepted if he made his home somewhere else, but he stuck to his roots and I think that was part of his downfall.

These lines are no less rich than James Hall's on the Southern frontiersman, but the connections between the quotations are just as strong. Albert Goldman wrote Elvis's family history (mostly ignoring Gladys's line in favor of Vernon's) as the story of rural degeneracy; from Hall to the anonymous Memphian, one can trace a degeneration of democratic values.

There is first a degeneration of the language common to educated Americans—originally, a language shaped by instruction in Latin, instruction that was inseparable from the ability of the founding fathers to articulate a creed of liberty and equality in words that still carry their full authority. The Memphian is readable, but there is a confusion in his syntax, and none of the drama or personality of Hall's prose. The present-day aristocrat can say what he means; unlike his cultural ancestor, he can't shape his meaning. And the degeneration of democratic language exposes a degeneration of democratic empathy. The privileged Memphian respects "Mr. Presley," but there is no hint that a poor-white-trash Elvis revealed to him the poverty of his own life, revealed the lack of fire and verve to which his every line is testimony. A lack of fire and verve is precisely what the frontiersman revealed to Hall, and it is precisely what, thirty years ago, Elvis Presley revealed to America at large.

In Colonel Parker's words, Elvis had a million dollars' worth of talent, then he had a million dollars—and he was still, as the liberal weekly the *Nation* recently said of Michael Jackson, taken as no more than confirmation of "the cliché that with luck and pluck any poor wretch can achieve fame and fortune." With Parker guarding the castle, it was a sure thing that Elvis would never grow up: never learn to ask questions, the answers to which were all of them ugly.

Dundy makes it plain that such a fate cannot be blamed on Gladys Presley. It's notorious that Gladys walked Elvis to and from school every day, first hand in hand, then behind him, then on the other side of the street, then hiding behind bushes to save him embarrassment; Dundy argues that this seeming wet blanket of mother love had two specific, valuable functions. Gladys made certain her boy would go to school and stay there; more vitally, as a woman who was herself deprived of serious education, a woman for whom a high school diploma was almost unthinkable, she was enacting a sort of "ceremony" of hope.

It's a moving concept, and Dundy brings it to life. She establishes that Elvis had great freedom of movement in Tupelo: from the age of eight he crossed town regularly, sometimes hitchhiking. He made himself a pest at radio station WELO and got himself on the air; he hung around country singer Mississippi Slim, no less questionable a character than any rounder, and sang on his radio show. Goldman, so scornful of Gladys as a walking quilt, would have used this information as proof that Gladys was *insufficiently* protective, but here it opens up the story. Dundy has done the research to back up words Stanley Booth wrote in 1968: Gladys was "the one, perhaps the only one, who had told [Elvis] throughout his life that even though he came from poor country people, he was just as good as anybody."

There is much more: such previously unreported incidents as Elvis hitching 240 miles in 1953 to Meridian, Mississippi, to enter a singing contest at the first Jimmie Rodgers "Father of Country Music" festival; the dating of his association with Sun bassist Bill Black to 1951, and accounts of their subsequent, pre-Sun jam sessions, to the point of a four-hour rehearsal on a single song. Dundy suggests it was almost certainly Arthur Crudup's "That's All Right," which in 1954 would become Elvis's first record—   113

Elvis powers through the imagination of a 16 year-old Mexican baby-sitter; as strange in Death as in life. Elvis fries down the door.

Gary Panter, pages from *Invasion of the Elvis Zombies*, 1984.

according to legend a studio accident, according to Dundy any-thing but.

That last note rings false; as an inversion of the just-fooling-around story it's simply too perfect. Dundy's great accomplishment is to have shown that the legend is also too perfect. The com-plexities and contradictions remain, but there is new flesh on them.

With Gary Panter's *Invasion of the Elvis Zombies*, the old flesh rots off. This is a work of comic-strip cartoon art: three tales run across the pages simultaneously. One is a collapsed-narrative al-legory in which Elvis's ghost—or corpse—turns into a swamp monster, dripping blood and slime like a creature from the black lagoon of cultural repression; one is a fairly rational *Twilight Zone*–style sitcom, where the thing returns to beg solace from two young girls. The last is only a face: you flip the bottom right corners

Elvis' knowledge of Brahmans is complete. He attaches himself with fussy rodent pleasure hump by hump to smear his face with fat and blood Rocky mountain spotted fever.

of the pages to follow its transmogrification from autopsy to nightmare.

To the question, did Elvis go to heaven, or did Elvis go to hell, Panter offers answers commensurate with the subject. His Elvis is too enormous, too voracious, too strange, too singular to join any known fate. Like ordinary history, ordinary religion gets Panter nowhere, and he explodes Dundy's book along with Priscilla's. Panter's Elvis is in limbo, from where he sallies forth according to his fancy—from where he is called forth, according to ours. His Elvis returns for love and revenge, he "packs in hordes of mud-rusty callgirls; Revelations that ground him for 150 years. Shrimps light up his feet. HOT CUTE DOLL a big man smelling for help," he devours the bodies of his fans, his mother appears naked, with four eyes and huge teeth, waving a broom to drive him off, he

115

Girls from all over the world come to take a bite out of Elvis. Happy ever after they shower him with laughter. He exploded with recognition. Wordlessly they tiptoe back. He waits with vinyl lips and mascara to repay them.

moves on—until we stop thinking about Elvis Presley, Panter seems to be saying, he cannot rest. He walks our hills in a long black veil: the black shadows around his eyes, one more legacy from Gladys. He walks his hills like Barbara Allen, Pretty Polly, Omie Wise, like all of those doomed Child-ballad maidens whose Scots-Irish melodies came South at the same time as Elvis's first American ancestors—and yet because he is a progenitor of our own time, of postwar wealth and pop culture modernism, he walks our streets like a demon in a drive-in movie: on Panter's last page, as a Mississippi Godzilla, rising out of a burning Safeway supermarket, immortal, undead. Dundy says Elvis sang "Barbara Allen" as a boy—one of those ancient songs, as Bob Dylan once described them, "about roses growing out of people's brains and lovers who are really geese and swans that turn into angels," music, he said, that was "too unreal to die . . . in that music is the only true, valid death you can feel today off a record player"—and one's first thought is, of course! And why didn't Elvis ever make an album of the old tunes he carried in his blood? Panter's question is, why didn't he ever make a horror movie? The questions make one answer: Child ballads were eighteenth- and nineteenth-century versions of our horror movies, and Elvis lived both.

Back to the bland: Lee Cotten's *All Shook Up—Elvis, Day by Day, 1954–77* is if nothing else almost certainly the longest rock nonbook ever published. What else is there to say about this 580-page log of dead facts, figures, dates, and places ("1962. SEPTEMBER. SEPT 4 [Tues.] Elvis and a crew of 100 from Metro-Goldwyn-Mayer arrived in Seattle to photograph scenes on location at the World's Fair. Elvis and his entourage stayed at the New Washington Hotel, in a fourteenth floor suite") except that—

Nodding off already? Buck up: there're fifteen years to go. I read through this book (no, I didn't read all of it) looking for a lone discord, a whisper of subjectivity, a taste of excess. I can't swear there's no such thing in *All Shook Up* (terrible title: this book has as much of "All Shook Up" in it as yesterday's hog futures chart), only that the format, stretched into an infinity of meaninglessness (most compendiums of this sort utilize an abbreviation code; this one, favoring "Metro-Goldwyn-Mayer" over "MGM," and even "fourteen" over "14," is actually [nodding off again, aren't you?] padded), dissolves the most insignificant facts into the most trivial.

Another Cotten epic (compiled with Howard A. DeWitt), *Jailhouse Rock: The Bootleg Records of Elvis Presley, 1970–1983*, has a pulse; illustrated with reproductions of sleeve art, cross-referenced, it's a consumer guide for the Elvis-fan version of the Trekkie. You can't read it any more than you can read *All Shook Up*, but there are wonders here: for example, the bootleg consisting solely of outtakes of "Can't Help Falling in Love," including the one where the King stutters and stammers all the way through the song. (I'd mention the title of the album, but I lost my place, and it'd take me weeks to find it again.) The real prize is lagniappe: on the last page, a transcription of the lyrics to "Jailhouse Rock" as they appeared on the cover of a Brazilian LP. This is Elvis dada: "Now I'm part of seven / Said my mama three / You use cute this Jail further ever did see / I show I'll be alive when you call for me / Come on to the Jail / Let's rock it wanna be."

Back to the weird, which isn't to say we aren't already there: with Elvis, blandness produces its own weirdness. Thomas Corboy's *Rock 'n' Roll Disciples* is a twenty-seven-minute documentary about Elvis fans; all the incomprehensible hysterics you see on television speak clearly here. Corboy focuses on Artie Mentz, an Elvis impersonator with the standard rap (not-a-job-but-a-calling); on Jerry and Judy Carroll, identical twins who won't say yes to guys who say no to the King; and on Frankie Horrocks, known to Memphis pilgrims as the Button Lady (she wears so many Elvis badges she clinks when she walks). In her forties, always smoking, a tough talker and an easy laugher, she is a woman of unconquerable dignity. Other people saying what she says might sound insane; she commands respect.

Intercut with Metz and the Carrolls, Horrocks tells her story: "November 14, 1966. The movie *Blue Hawaii*, and I fell in love, and I was a *newlywed*. Ha! I told my husband I wanted a divorce. 'I'm in love, and it's not with you.' " Eventually, her husband cut her loose: "Item number two [on his divorce petition] was 'Excessive devotion to Elvis Presley.' And I said, 'I love it!'

"He was someone who took up 99 percent of my time," Horrocks says, "and my money. And yet the thought of killing myself [after Elvis's death] never even crossed my mind." She went to Memphis as soon as she heard the news, and has lived there since; she left two teenage daughters behind. Her youngest daughter was already dead, murdered by a man who pleaded insanity, was set free, and killed again. That girl was Horrocks's only soulmate in her family: another Elvis fan. Horrocks took her to an Elvis concert, Elvis brought her up out of the crowd, kissed her; she refused to wash the dress she'd worn. Horrocks buried her in it, a copy of "Burning Love" in her folded hands.

118

The Carroll twins are certain that (1) Elvis is not dead, and (2) Elvis is their father. It's spooky—they look far more like him than Lisa Marie does. They finish each other's sentences like Huey, Dewey, and Louie; you get the idea they have the routine down pat; there's just the slightest sensation that they're putting you on. But not with Horrocks. The Carroll women have a blithe, cinematic sensuality: if they believe (1) and (2) you might be excused for imagining it's because they're into incest. Horrocks is no kid; if she lives in a fantasy world, her overwhelming pride makes it seem like real life. She offers just the smallest hint that she herself once slept with Elvis—fucked him, as she'd say if she wasn't on camera. She doesn't dwell on the possibility; what she wants to talk about is the nature of fandom.

Any normal, red-blooded American woman that loves him is a liar if she said, "I would *not* want to go to bed with Elvis Presley."

No, I take that back. I met a woman who said if she was given the opportunity of making love to Elvis or having him sing to her, she would want him to sing to her. And I looked at her and I said, "You're *sick*."

Personally, *I'd* want him to sing *while* he was making love.

As she speaks, the video shows her posed against the statue of Elvis that now stands in Memphis, her hand cupping its crotch. The tableau is reminiscent of nothing so much as the statues of Catholic saints that in present-day Europe good Christian women straddle in pagan ecstasy, telling anyone who asks that their mothers said it was a good way to ensure fertility. Horrocks negates the neurotic sanctity of so many pious female Elvis fanatics; compared to the women who've told us they've thrown over their lives for Elvis "because he loved people," she's a psychoanalyst in a nunnery. You can't laugh at her; you can't even blink.

Then there is Ed McClanahan, born in Kentucky, the sort of professional Southerner created by the impulse of the American media to ghettoize whatever is not bland enough to reach into every sector of national life without changing any of it. In *Famous*   119

People I Have Known, a collection of pieces about stuff he did and persons he met over the last thirty years, McClanahan thus finds it necessary to say such things as, "Like everybody else who lived in California during the 1960s, I Went Through a Phase. I grew me a mustache and a big wig, got me some granny glasses and pointy-toed elf boots and bell-bottom britches"—but, he wants you to know with his I-grew-me's and his britches, he's a good old boy at heart. His book escapes itself only with its longest chapter, the history of one "Little Enis," an early Elvis imitator, a man who started out just a year or so after "Heartbreak Hotel" and who pressed on, past Elvis's death, through the 1970s, until he too died. "Little Enis," you see—Elvis was "Elvis the Pelvis," and he was "Enis the Penis."

Faced with a man whose whole life was a joke worse than any he can tell, McClanahan drops his posturing. When he says he's drunk, for the first time you feel it; when he rocks out, you do too. In this account of a fat, ugly nobody, who cannot quite imagine inventing himself but who can imagine turning into someone else, is the best sense in print of why so many people care so much about Elvis imitators: it's the willingness to settle. When one cannot have the truth, one still wants it, and so one will accept a play in which, for a stray moment—after midnight, full of booze and pills—a representation of the truth sparks emotions that cannot be distinguished from the emotions produced by an apprehension of the thing itself. McClanahan makes the reader understand that, in some crummy bar, a broken-down fake in his fat, ugly forties could produce a response that Elvis, in his fat, ugly forties, or even in his slim, addled thirties, could not. Elvis made people want something; when he couldn't give it, they still wanted it and, in stray moments, fakes could provide it, and make the people who got it feel confirmed. Watching from his seat in the bar, McClanahan writes out the truth that a representation can make people feel as deeply as whatever it is the representation represents.

It's an unsettling notion, confusing—and what it reveals is not the depth of the Elvis-imitator's imitation, but the scope of the liberation Elvis himself was unable to permit himself to portray.

As a fake, the Elvis imitator can do anything: walk onstage drunk, fall over, talk dirty, fondle women in the audience, throw up. Everyone knows it isn't real, that it isn't really happening, and so the dispensation, one's distance from one's own desires, is sealed.

What Elvis did was not only thrilling, it was painful. With every true seizure of desire, every fan had to give up something just as valuable: the comfort of rules. The performance of the Elvis imitator sparks the emotions the real thing could spark—and through the strictures of what-is and what-is-not altogether separates those emotions from their possible consequences. Elvis himself took no prisoners: he released you into the world. The Elvis imitator, himself the prisoner of a representation he never made, makes you love your chains. "If only, if only," he makes you say—and all the emotions of release come forth. But Elvis did not say "if only." In his best music he destroyed the qualifier, and replaced it with a negation that was also an affirmation: your life is empty, but there is another life. It was thrilling and terrifying—no wonder so many prefer the Elvis imitator to Elvis, irreducible in his absolute subjectivity. Drunk in a dive with an old Little Enis singing "It's Now or Never," McClanahan gets it across.

Back to the mystery. Nick Cave is an Australian rock 'n' roll singer working in England; his LP *The Firstborn Is Dead* is a sort of Deep South concept album that begins with a mystical version of the birth of Elvis and Jesse Garon and ends with an elegy to country bluesman Blind Lemon Jefferson. The opening number, "Tupelo," sets the tone: it's pretentious, pounding, absurdly overblown, and it grabs you by the throat. Based on a John Lee Hooker blues of the same name, Cave's "Tupelo" is instantly biblical, a torrent of incantations that drive all rational objections straight out of mind. A storm is raging, then a flood. The Beast—the Devil—comes up; God is missing. Time stands still; the laws of nature are suspended. "And the black rain came down. Water water everywhere. Where no bird can fly no fish can swim. No fish can swim Until the King is born! Until the King is born! In Tupelo! Tupelo-o-o! Til the King is born in Tupelo!"

The identification of Elvis with Jesus has been a secret theme of the Elvis story at least since 1956; since Elvis's death it has been no secret at all. In 1982 in Memphis, Sam Phillips told a crowd of fans and followers that the two most important events in American history were the birth of Jesus and the birth of Elvis Presley. The audience didn't know how to respond—was this blasphemy, or the truth? Cave raises such questions and escapes them, barrels through them. His "Tupelo" takes its energy not from the gospels but from the black arts that hang over the Mississippi Delta blues like a traveling cloud: Cave seems to be less making the music than carried away by it, less a performer than a messenger. You forget everything you think you know about Elvis Presley; the story begins at the beginning. "Well Saturday gives what Sunday steals. And a child is born on his brother's heels. Come Sunday morn the firstborn is dead. In a shoe-box tied with a ribbon of red. Tupelo-o-o! Hey Tupelo! In a shoe-box tied with a ribbon of red." Cave combines parable with nursery rhyme, shoots the hybrid forth with hoodoo power, and it's not easy to catch: plenty of first-rank black American pop musicians have described entire careers without a touch of hoodoo conjure. Some, like Junior Walker—as a session man contributing a hired saxophone solo to Foreigner's "Urgent"—caught it only once, and in the oddest places. But Cave has it—or, as the game goes, it has him.

The question of did-he-go-to-heaven-or-did-he-go-to-hell falls away, replaced by a more earthly riddle: can the hoodoo Cave puts into Elvis's story—here, his *tale*—be found in Elvis's music? There are instants—the helpless rush of the singing in the last choruses of "Good Rockin' Tonight," perhaps—but all in all the music seems more rooted in the church, in a lust for status, in the Hollywood movies Elvis saw as a teenager. Hoodoo is not release; it is fear subsumed into will. And yet it is undeniable that the cultural transformation Elvis Presley wrought across America, and then across the world, cannot simply be traced back to the familiar. There was an element in that transformation that those who were transformed could neither resist nor integrate into the cultural matrix they brought to the event, and thus those people had to transform the cultural matrix: the world had to change. Was it hoodoo?

Cave offers no answer; *The Firstborn Is Dead* is a rite, not an analysis. But Michael Ventura has no doubts. His *Shadow Dancing in the U.S.A.* is a collection of extremist critiques of all sorts of American culture—video games, sexual practices, the movies, Las Vegas, "the sixties," marriage, dance, high technology—centered by a sixty-page essay called "Hear That Long Snake Moan." This is a passionate, sometimes burning history of the roots of rock 'n' roll and jazz in kidnapped African religion (voodoo or vodun in the Caribbean, hoodoo in the American South) and Celtic religion (Irish slaves sent to the Caribbean in the seventeenth century in a last English attempt to Christianize Ireland by deporting its pagans). Ventura sees what he calls "Christianism" as a war on the body, and thus on the soul; his Elvis is the avatar of a war against Christianism. The concept is heretical—obviously, Elvis himself would have been the first to refuse it. But the explanation makes sense.

Elvis's singing was so extraordinary because you could *hear* the moves, infer the moves, in his singing. No white man and few blacks had ever sung so completely with the whole body.

Elvis, before the Army, before 1959, was something truly extraordinary: a white man who seemed, to the rest of us, to appear out of nowhere with moves that most white people had never imagined, let alone seen. His legs weren't solidly planted then, as they would be years later. They were always in motion. Often he'd rise on his toes, seem on the verge of some impossible groin-propelled leap, then twist, shimmy, dip, and shake in some direction you wouldn't have expected. You *never* expected it. Every inflection was matched, accented, *harmonized* by an inflection of muscle. As though the voice couldn't sing unless the body moved. . . .

Nobody had ever seen a white boy move like that. He was a flesh-and-blood rent in white reality. A gash in the nature of Western things.

123

Through him, or through his image, a whole culture started to pass from its most strictured, fearful years to our unpredictably fermentive age—a jangled, discordant feeling, at once ultra-modern and primitive. . . .

Ventura goes on to detail the role of the pantheistic loa gods in Haitian voodoo, to explicate the confusion between one's possession by the loa and the continuing autonomy of the loa itself (we are back with Nick Cave's Beast, with the confusion of just what, or just who, is turning Tupelo on 8 January 1935 into a maelstrom), and then speaks as plainly as Sam Phillips in Memphis in 1982: "The Voodoo rite of possession by the god *became the standard of American performance in rock 'n' roll.*" Think about it: Ventura is not saying that American rock 'n' rollers became voodoo adepts, but that, by a certain cultural transference, a particular test of religious commitment became a generalized test of aesthetic power. Ventura sums up:

Texas singer and songwriter Butch Hancock comments on Presley's historic appearance on the "Ed Sullivan Show": "Yeah, that was the dance that everybody forgot. It was the dance that was so strong it took an entire civilization to forget it. And ten seconds to remember it."

All those who were changed by such events—all those who were changed, scared, insulted, thrilled, appalled, which is not to include millions who were not even born when the event Butch Hancock speaks of took place, but who live in the world that came forth as a result—are still trying to understand what it took ten seconds to remember, or to deny it. In Ventura's book, almost the whole of our culture is presented as a cover-up of what Elvis Presley exposed—and so it can be no surprise that the pursuit of Elvis's legacy, its marketing and its celebration, produces cover-ups of its own. But what exactly it is that needs to be covered up remains as much a mystery as it ever was—and thus the answers to questions that never quite take final shape move inevitably into a cultural wilderness, unmapped and unnamed. To me, it remains wonderful that we are still faced with questions we are only beginning to learn how to ask; that "So much for Elvis Presley" is a sentence no serious person has yet been able to write with a straight face.

1987

Ten Years After:
Death on the Installment Plan

We got into a fight when Elvis died . . .
We ran out to some bar in town
Some big-mouth drunk was makin' jokes
Puttin' Elvis down

My baby gave him fair warnin'
Everybody said
But when he sang "Don't Be Cruel"
Baby lost his cool
And shot him dead

—"Listening to Elvis," sung by Syd Straw,
written by Scott Kempner, 1985

The '50s I remember were pretty tough, uptight—and I'm trying to make the '50s lead into the '60s and show how things opened up, and people's reactions to that. Why a guy like Kerouac would become so important, and Presley, who freed us.
—Ralph Bakshi, on his film *Hey Good Looking*, 1982

They're talkin' again about how to survive nuclear wars. But it was that kind of talk, in the Fifties, that caused rock & roll to emerge. It was that kind of talk that created the necessity for Marlon Brando and James Dean, and the necessity for young people to need—not like, but *need*—

Elvis Presley.
—Peter Wolf, 1982

Since leaving Ghana 10 years ago, Elvis Johnson-Idan, 36, has lived in the north London borough of Brent, where he currently presides over the park department.

He recently received word that the former monarch of his Ghanian tribe, the Fantis, had died. This makes you king, said the message from Ghana.

Power over 10,000 subjects doesn't seem to mean much to the man who will become King Elvis. He will return to London after his coronation. "I'm doing a very important job here," he said, "and I like it very much."

—Leah Garchik, San Francisco Chronicle, 1986

> nine heroes later i cannot watch any more tv.
> knife, I mean life, is portrayed so funny.
> even the fifteen year old hooker
> on barney miller talks in punch lines.
> prostitution is so funny,
> maybe we should all try it . . .
>
> spa king. ktell presents
> "elvis sings at his own funeral"
> —author unknown, c. 1984

> Can't you just imagine
> Digging up the King
> Begging him to sing
> About those heavenly mansions
> Jesus mentioned
> —Warren Zevon, "Jesus Mentioned," 1982

You don't even have to imagine it: he's been dug up again and again since he went into the ground ten years ago. Of course he sings at his own funeral, a ceremony that has yet to end—who'd you expect, Little Richard?

How does he sound? Great, if you listen to the new CDs. As a friend put it, punching up "Jailhouse Rock" and quoting Roland Barthes, "You can actually hear 'the grain of the voice.' " But if you listen to Bono Hewson's shadow-play impersonation on U2's tune "Elvis Presley and America," he sounds terrible: real. This is Elvis in the hour before he died, fixed forever, last words, the aural equivalent of what you see on the page of the King's demented letter to the president, asking to be made a "Federal Agent at Large" so he can help stop "The Drug Culture"—

expressed my concern for our country. The Drug Culture, the Hippie Elements, the SDS, Black Panthers, etc. do not consider me as their enemy or as they call it the Establishment. I call it America and

—not the grain of the voice, just the garble of dope. Zevon finishes his song, his voice descending line by line: "He went walking on the water / He went walking on the water / He went walking on the water / With his pills."

Both Bono and Zevon are cursing: cursing what happened to Elvis, and cursing Elvis for letting it happen, for betraying the faith they placed in him. In an interview with Bill Flanagan, Bono explained:

This book by Albert Goldman made Elvis out as being the rock & roll idiot. The book made me very, very angry. Because I believe that Elvis Presley was a genius. He didn't express himself the way the middle classes do, which is with wordplay and being able to express his actions and reactions. He acted on gut instinct and expressed himself by the way he held the microphone. . . . If you read the books that Elvis read

128

—pause over that line, "If you read the books that Elvis read"; Bono has done research—

they were books of a man who was unsure of himself intellectually. When he *should* have been sure of himself. He was dragging himself down. . . . I believe the essence of any performer is gut instinct, "and you love though no one told you to. You know but no one told you how." Because it's all in you, it's instinct. That's what Elvis Presley's about. And yet the music business tries to make you explain yourself and explain your actions and reactions. And Elvis couldn't and felt that he should have been able to. And I think that tore at him, and it shouldn't have torn at him because he was better than all those people. He's better than Albert Goldman, and Elvis Presley could say more in *somebody else's song* than Albert Goldman could say in any book. . . . Elvis had the wisdom that makes wise men foolish.

The maggots that first crawled out of his eyes are grandparents to the nth degree, but still people cannot stop talking, can't stop trying to understand. Bruce Springsteen, for example, speaking from the stage, remembering Elvis on the *Ed Sullivan Show* in 1956: "It was like he came along and whispered a dream in everybody's ear and then we dreamed it." Dreamed what? "The American dream," presumably, a now-horrible cliché best summed up by A. Whitney Brown on a recent *Saturday Night Live*:

And what *is* the American dream?

It's different things to different people. To a farmer, it's a bountiful harvest, that he can sell, for a lotta money. To a photographer, it's a beautiful picture, that he can sell, for a lotta money. To a soldier, it's becoming a general, so that he can sell weapons to a foreign country, for a lotta money.

But maybe I can best express the American dream in a story. It's about a kid who grew up in Tupelo, Mississippi, in the early 1950s. He was a poor kid, but he had a rockin' guitar, some flashy clothes, and a wiggle in his hips—and he had that certain something, called "talent."

Of course, he never made a nickel, because he was black, but two years later Elvis Presley made a fortune doing the same thing . . .

Which isn't what he meant at all, Springsteen goes on to say: ". . . the TV, the cars, the houses—that's not the American dream. Those are the booby prizes. And if you fall for them—if, when you achieve them, you believe this is the end in and of itself— then you've been suckered in. Because those are the consolation prizes, if you're not careful, for selling yourself out or lettin' the best of yourself slip away."

The Elvis Presley we read about in filler items in the daily papers is the booby prize. No, says media widow Priscilla (divorced from Elvis before he died, she can't quite be the real thing), it isn't true that she and daughter Lisa Marie have turned over the entire Presley estate to the Church of Scientology, though the Church has brought both mother and daughter a peace beyond price. On the other hand, Priscilla confides, it is true that having already chopped up Elvis's Bel Air house and bronzed the bricks and sold them at Graceland, she is now ready to unload the furniture, tables on which the hands once placed a Pepsi, chairs into which the corpus actually sank (probably she didn't bother to have 'em dry-cleaned; maybe there'll be a telltale stain?). The prices are high, but . . . "I never saw such junk in my life," said a fan. "My God, what would Elvis think?"

Over at the Berkeley Psychic Institute, also known as the Church of the Divine Man, they're working on the problem. In fact, they go to the source almost every day: Elvis has been channeled.

"I think that Elvis Presley will never be solved," Nick Tosches wrote in *Country* in 1977, just after Elvis's death. Tosches had just finished celebrating "Blue Moon of Kentucky," the flipside of Elvis's first record, cut with Sam Phillips in Memphis on 6 July 1954: "Like a young boxer after his first professional knockout, Presley is dizzy with the confirmation of his prowess. 'Blue Moon of Kentucky' is daring to the point of mania. It is Elvis walking on steel blades, through orange-white flames, invincible with the knowledge he sees in Sam's eyes, hears in his own voice, and feels in his own flushed skin; the knowledge that right now, this moment, he, Elvis Aron Presley, is the greatest singer in Memphis and the universe." Never put better, that was what the world responded to, the leaping sense that in an instant the world could be turned upside down. "Nothing," Tosches wrote of Elvis leaving that first realized moment, "not sex, not the eyes of bank tellers, would ever again disarm with its mystery." That is the wisdom that makes wise men foolish, but the gnosis that dissolves all mystery is its own mystery—what is that leaping sense of transformation, exactly? Where does it come from? Where does it go? Is it real at all?—and that mystery is what people are still talking about. It's what Tosches was talking about, what he said would never be solved: the fact that, emerging from the orange-white flames of "Blue Moon of Kentucky," Elvis immediately "declared his idol to be Dean Martin, the 37-year-old Italian pop singer from Steubenville, Ohio." This, Tosches said, "is modestly terrifying."

Back at the Church of the Divine Man, where terror is merely a hole in the aura of the insufficiently evolved, there are no questions without answers, no problems that cannot be solved. Here one can find people who have finally closed the split between Dean Martin and "Blue Moon of Kentucky," casting it in the less esoteric terms of "the Rebel and the Good Boy." This, reports the *Psychic Reader*, is the "duality" that has dominated Presley iconography for thirty years, and Elvis's soul since 8 January 1935, when he emerged from the womb of Gladys Presley twinned to the corpse of Jesse Garon—whose spirit would not die. As Elvis told Bill Falcone, his channeler, both he

Drew Friedman, cartoon, 1987.

and his brother struggled for control of the surviving body. Elvis the Rebel (the Jesse spirit) wore sideburns and wild pink and black clothes and worshipped James Dean. Elvis the Good Boy (the original spirit) was deeply religious. . . . The struggle between the two spirits in Elvis's body only intensified as Elvis became a star. The Jesse Garon being, the destroyer, started to shoot out TV sets during violent outbursts. He surrounded himself with southern buddies and developed an obsession for guns, becoming increasingly paranoid as his strange, cloistered night-life was termed decadent and maniacal. The [true] Elvis spirit took uppers, downers, and painkillers, in pill form and injections, to try to get some relief . . . the Jesse being was [the true Elvis said before he died] "some kind of sex maniac," bragging to his stepmother that he had slept with more than 1,000 women.

Those women meant nothing to the "true" Elvis, whose greatest love of his life was his mother Gladys. . . . In a psychic reading held at the Berkeley Psychic Institute, Gladys Presley was channeled through Rev. Rose Letsgo. When asked why Elvis died at the same time as she, almost to the day of the year [14 August 1958], Gladys replied that "We were Siamese twins in a past life."

So there you have it. The real Elvis liked Dean Martin and went on to a life of torment and pain. The false Elvis made "Blue Moon of Kentucky" and had a good time. The corollary is that rebellion, like the rebel, is born dead.

For the moment, this is where the story stops: returned to the supposed piety of Elvis's beginnings, to Jesus's mansions (though in this Father's house there is only one), or to the occult, where Elvis ended, to the spiritualist tracts that occupied him in his last days (he was said to be reading *The Face of Jesus*, a book about the Shroud of Turin, when he died*). Both sides of the story are fecund: Warren Zevon's "Jesus Mentioned" is a wonderful song, and occultism reveals the secret contours of the story, of our help-less commitment to it. Versions appear everywhere, as in a recent *Village Voice* article on Neal Jimenez, scenarist of *River's Edge*,

---

* So it was reported at the time; in *The Death of Elvis: What Really Happened* (1991), Charles C. Thompson II and James P. Cole argue the book was in fact *Sex and Psychic Energy*, an astrological sex manual.

and also of an unshot screenplay "called *Son of Elvis*—about a girl who pushes to the front of an Elvis concert in '56, touches the King's finger, becomes pregnant as a result, and has a son who must bear the burden of his lineage some 20 years later." One can laugh at the Church of the Divine Man, but Jimenez is working on the same level, and who wouldn't want to see his script come to life?

This is where the story has to go, now: underground, into fantasy, in retreat from the spectacle that is about to unfold. On August 16, on the tenth anniversary of Elvis Presley's Death Day, untold thousands from around the world will gather in Memphis. Every network will run a spot or a special. ("Not a smirk story," a producer for CBS's *West 57th Street* told me. "We're going serious.") There will be cable television documentaries and retrospectives (at least three are in the works); the cover of *Newsweek* is on hold. There will even be *Elvis: Undercover*, a comic book from Mad Dog Graphics, in which Elvis's dream of fighting "The Drug Culture" will finally come true.

Catherine Deeter, illustration for Mark Shipper, *How to be Ecstatically Happy 24 Hours a Day for the Rest of Your Life* (809 Productions), 1986.

The media coverage will be so bloated, and so empty, that people may finally begin to turn away. Elvis Presley will be blown up, splattered into a million fragments. Right now, perhaps, each of those fragments still retains a link to a totality, to a story much bigger than that of one person, one time; after August 16 each fragment may be just a piece of a story that can no longer be put back together, that can no longer be told.

It's time for it. The stories about Elvis are old now; they've been told too many times. Almost every recording has been issued; the chest of relics is almost empty. Save for scattered cults, most of them in the South, made up of working-class people not unlike Elvis (people who cannot, as Bono said, "explain their actions and reactions"), or in Europe, made up of people for whom Elvis is still fundamentally exotic, people may cease to wonder. The books will stop selling: even the likes of Lucy de Barbin and Dary Matera's *Are You Lonesome Tonight? The Untold Story of Elvis Presley's One True Love—and the Child He Never Knew*. Even that. *We* will rest in peace.

As for Elvis, he will become a poster: as fixed, as simple, and as sterile as the movie-still posters of Marlon Brando (leaning against his motorcycle in *The Wild One*), James Dean (leaning against his car in *Rebel Without a Cause*), and Marilyn Monroe (skirts billowing up in *The Seven Year Itch*). In place of the unfathomable multiplicity Elvis Presley has signified for three decades, there will be a single, uninteresting image, at once specific and generic, signifying nothing.

For the first time, Elvis will be really dead. For the first time, people will stop talking. There will be nothing left to say. And then, twenty years later, when the people who stopped talking have passed on, when the specter that this year will lay to rest has had the sleep it needs, when all the reissues of obscure Sun outtakes have been forgotten, when even Desirée Presley ("the Child He Never Knew") has forgotten, someone like Neal Jimenez will make his movie, and it will all come back.

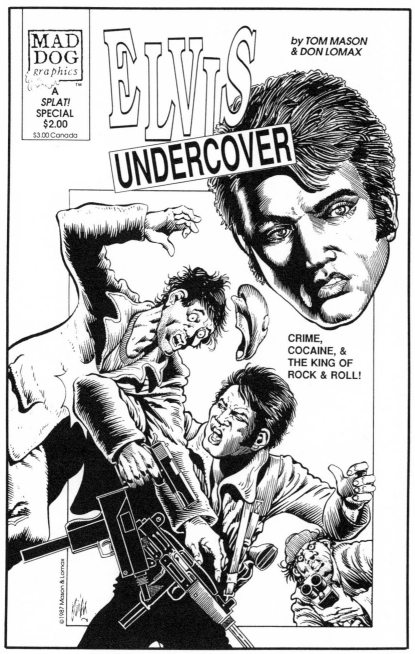

Tom Mason and Don Lomax, dummy cover for *Elvis: Undercover*, with press release (Mad Dog Graphics), 1987.

P.O. Box 931686 Hollywood, CA 90093   213/464-2932

FOR IMMEDIATE RELEASE

Elvis´s Ghost Cancels Comic Book

Hollywood--The ghost of Elvis Presley has been credited with the cancellation of Elvis: Undercover, a one-shot satirical comic that is no longer forthcoming from Mad Dog Graphics.

Says Mad Dog publisher Jan Strnad: "I had just fixed a peanut butter sandwich and was settling in for some light reading. I´d placed the sandwich on the coffeetable, stacked some platters on my Silvertone record player with the tilt-down turntable, and had just begun paging through Are You Lonesome Tonight. The soundtrack to Girl Happy was barely through the title cut when suddenly the Silvertone went dead. The temperature dropped fifteen degrees, and I knew something strange was about to happen.

"A phosphorescent shape appeared before me. It was vague and wavering, like heat shimmers over hot Memphis blacktop, but there was no mistaking the cocky stance, the white jumpsuit, or the slow resonant voice that spoke my name. I knew immediately that the apparition before me was the King of Rock and Roll.

"He spoke deliberately, with excruciating politeness, and wished me luck with all my projects...save one. I knew he was referring to Elvis: Undercover, but he was just too polite to

-more-

136

mention it by name. My tongue stumbled around in my mouth trying in vain to form the words "First Amendment," but a mystical Spell of Inarticulation had seized me and I was unable to explain the moral imperative behind publishing a book ridiculing his life and character.

"Suddenly the whole project seemed trivial and meanspirited. I felt ashamed. I forced my unwilling lips to speak, and I promised Elvis that I would cancel the book he´d travelled so far not to mention.

"He stretched out a shimmering hand. ´Thanks,´ he said. ´Here--this is for you.´ I reached out and Elvis placed a small object in my palm, closing my fingers over it tightly. ´Don´t look until I´m gone,´ he said, and then he faded from sight.

"The lights went up, the stereo came on, and I was left wondering: Had the visitation really happened, or was it all just a crazy dream? Slowly I opened my hand. There in my palm was the gift Elvis had given me--a tiny droplet of sweat, sealed in a genuine plastic vial.

"I collapsed into my chair with the precious vial clasped to my chest. I looked around the room to see if anything had changed, if The King had left any other mementos of his visit. I regarded the empty plate on my coffeetable, and I smiled.

"Elvis had taken my peanut butter sandwich."

-30-

137

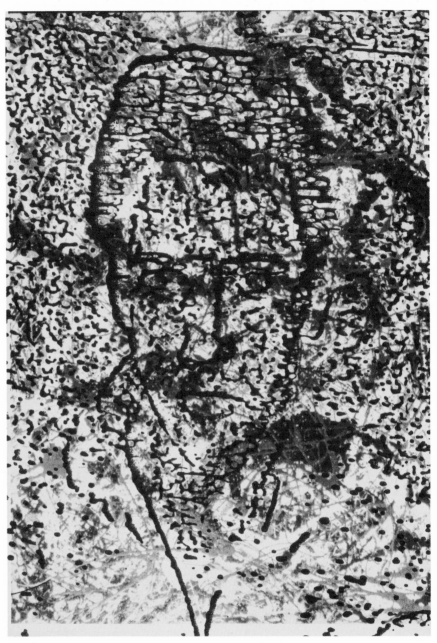

Mekons, *Portrait of Elvis Presley in the Style of Jackson Pollock*, No. 12, laser origination by Chila Kumari Burman, 1989.

Still Dead

1982

The Man Who Wasn't Elvis

At 3 A.M., inside Graceland, "Elvis Presley lay in his blue cotton pajamas, dreaming. A small bubble of saliva burst softly at the corner of his lips, and, breathing heavily, he turned. It was the same old dream."

He walked through Tupelo in the late afternoon on a summer's day toward the home of the virgin Evangeline. He was smiling as he turned a corner and entered a street where lush hackberry trees swallowed the sun. There was the house of her father, where she waited, wrapped in that magic, unholy thing from her mama's bottom drawer.

He felt a chill. He was naked. Pleasance became dread, and he flushed with panic. He would retreat across town, where his mother was not dead, and there fetch his clothes. If he hurried, there was time. He took a shortcut through a backyard that he recognized, but he was soon lost, running scared in a strange, unfriendly place until he came to a meadow like none he had ever seen, and afternoon became night and the meadow became endless and he screamed.

It's the telephone, the guard calling. Jerry Lee Lewis has arrived, demanding to be let in, showing his pistol. " 'Git on that damn house phone and call him! Who the hell does that sonofabitch think he is? Doesn't wanna be disturbed! He ain't no damn better'n anybody else.' "

Elvis motherfucking Presley—his heart hastened—setting up there in that goddamn mansion pretending he's God, and all he is is some fat old dope addict who dyes his hair like a goddamn woman. . . . To the grave, to the grave, to the grave. He almost laughed, but instead spat in disgust, then commenced howling anew. He did not relent, and the guard went to the phone.

The police were called, and Lewis was taken to jail. It was the twenty-third of November, 1976.

Thus the opening scene of Nick Tosches's *Hellfire: The Jerry Lee Lewis Story*, a typical scene: the way it should have been pulled against the way it was. It is the finest book ever written about a rock 'n' roll performer—nothing else comes close. But that is hardly all it is. Sooner or later, *Hellfire* will be recognized as an American classic.

In outline, "The Jerry Lee Lewis Story" is well known. Born in Ferriday, Louisiana, in 1935, Lewis was a hellion whose soul was pitched between the threats of the Holy Ghost and the charms of the devil—the latter taking the form of boogie-woogie piano. He stole, he preached, he went to Bible school, he was expelled from Bible school, he made music, and in 1957 Sun Records released his version of "Whole Lotta Shakin' Goin' On," a record that has not left the radio, or the mind of anyone who has ever heard it, in over a quarter of a century. Lewis became an international star. Almost immediately, the news of his marriage to his thirteen-year-old second cousin, Myra Gale Brown—it was his third marriage, and his second bigamy—destroyed his career.

Thrown back into the honky tonks, Lewis continued to perform and became addicted to pills and alcohol. In 1968 he made a deal with the mostly Southern, mostly God-fearing part of white America: he would, on record if not on stage, abjure music of sin—rock 'n' roll—in favor of music of guilt—country. He became a star for the second time. Before long he was a big enough star to do as he pleased, and he again recorded rock 'n' roll. But the years of dissipation and profligacy, and the old war between heaven and

141

Dave Abramson, collage from *Ahunka Lisa Marie* (Clambake Press), 1988.

hell, caught up, and once more his life collapsed around him. Time and again he was arrested, sued, divorced, hospitalized; his property was seized by the Internal Revenue Service, and he buried the second of two sons. When he entered a Memphis hospital in 1981, newspapers across the country reported that he was not expected to live; some even printed his obituary. When he did leave the hospital, he announced that from that day on he would use his God-given talent only to praise God. It was a promise he had first made as a teenager, and no one expected him to keep it.

Out of these materials, which are both commonplace and the stuff of legend, Nick Tosches has made a book that can be read along with Benjamin Franklin's *Autobiography*, Parson Weems's

Life of Washington, William Herndon's *Life of Lincoln*, and Van Wyck Brooks's *The Ordeal of Mark Twain*. It is as well a book that sent me back to Michael Wigglesworth's Puritan poem "The Day of Doom" ("They have their wish whose Souls perish with Torments in Hell-fire," Wigglesworth wrote in 1661, "Who rather choose their Souls to lose, than leave a loose desire"), and to Faulkner—to "Barn Burning," *Absalom, Absalom!*, and especially "Compson: 1699–1945," the postscript to *The Sound and the Fury* ("Who loved not the idea of the incest he would not commit, but some Presbyterian concept of its eternal punishment")—sent me back in search of the sources of Tosches's voice.

Hellfire has no truck with irony, that alibi of desiccated modernism. It is instead a strict and elegant rendering of perhaps the oldest and most enduring version of the American story: having blessed America above all other communities, God will judge its members more harshly. It is a notion that has produced much of the best and much of the worst in American life; it has led as surely to the Puritan witch trials and to the so-called Christian right of our day as to the compassion and terror in Lincoln's Second Inaugural Address. On this ground, Wigglesworth and Faulkner meet; they meet Jerry Lee Lewis, who at first refused to sing "Great Balls of Fire" because he recognized the song as an obscene blasphemy. At the same time, Tosches's book joins a special and peculiarly unexamined tradition of American biography. Like the books by Franklin, Weems, Herndon, and Brooks, and like our best nineteenth-century novels, it is a poetic, imaginative statement that means less to illuminate the American predicament than to judge it. *Hellfire* is not so much a "true story"—though no book could be more scrupulous about dates, places, record labels, crimes; about getting the story straight—as an implacable tract.

In contrast to the doorstop genre that has taken over American biography, where the life of the most trivial figure is excavated down to its most meaningless detail, Tosches's book is small and short. Like the biographies mentioned above, it is both an argument about values—where they come from, where they lead—and an example of the first American literary genre, the sermon. What makes the book so strange and so compelling is that the sermon comes not from some fixed, eternal set of religious values, like the sermons Lewis's first cousin Jimmy Swaggart, the TV evangelist, has often delivered on the subject of Jerry Lee, but from a transmutation of such values: from inside Lewis himself. It is a sermon in which the cadences of Lewis's life and the cadences of sin and salvation have created their own, new rhythms. *Hellfire* is the Jerry Lee Lewis story not as he might want it to be told—no matter how formally honest he might be, revealing every last legal and moral crime—but as a judgment he might dream, and from which he cannot awake.

Thus Tosches's language passes back through Faulkner, and back through preachers like Wigglesworth, to their own source: the Bible. Tosches weaves the most prosaic, seemingly anomalous details—chart positions of Lewis's records, copyright data, particulars of marriage licenses, dates of barnstorming rock 'n' roll tours—into that language, until *Hellfire* reads like nothing so much as twentieth-century Apocrypha. Tosches starts carefully, building the Lewis genealogy without ornamental portents or omens, describing without melodrama the arrival of Pentecostalism and the plaguelike outbreak of glossolalia in young Jerry Lee's hometown of Ferriday, then dropping flashing, seemingly classical lines here and there—"[He] slowly fell to that place where fame repeats its own name"—until the reader is ready for a passage like this one, ready to accept it at face value, with all the irony a reader might have brought to it burned off:

The booze and the pills stirred the hell within him and made him to utter hideous peals. At times he withdrew into his own shadow, brooding upon all manner of things—abominable, unutterable, and worse. At times he stalked and ranted in foul omnipotence, commanding those about him as Belial his minions. He was the Killer and he was immortal—damned to be, for as long as there were good and evil to be torn between in agony. He would sit backstage in a thousand dank nightclubs, and he would know this, and he would swallow more pills and wash them

144

down with three fingers more of whiskey, and he would know it even more. He would walk like a man to the stage, with his Churchill in one hand and his water glass of whiskey in the other, and he would beckon those before him, mortals, made not as he to destruction from the womb; he would beckon them to come, to stand with him awhile at the brink of hell. Then he would be gone into the ancient night, to more pills and more whiskey, to where the black dogs never ceased barking and dawn never broke; he would go there.

This is hardly the only sort of prose in *Hellfire*—just as common is "The hit records continued to come for Jerry Lee throughout 1970, and his concert price rose to $10,000 a night"—but this prose at once defines the book's anchor and its weight. The use of the semicolon; the devastating close with that endlessly reverberating "he would go there"; the placement of the biblical "and he would know this," brought down to an earth we can feel beneath our feet with the sardonic, no-hope smile of "and he would know it even more"—this, from a man whose previous book, *Country*, was just a little too hip, is bedrock American writing.

The strength, commitment, and sensitivity to rhythm in the writing provides the necessary credence for the context Tosches fashions: a struggle between old-time, fundamentalist religion and modern-day celebrity, between the wish or the will never to "leave a loose desire" and the consciousness that such a wish demands the destruction of the body and the soul. The context in turn makes sense of Lewis's story and links it to a story all Americans share, if only in pieces.

The question of making sense of the story, and establishing the reader's link to it, is especially alive in comparison to Albert Goldman's biography of Elvis. In *Hellfire*, crimes far worse than any Goldman dug up for Presley hum through the pages: a teenage Jerry Lee tries to kill his little sister, he commits bigamy and countless infidelities, he buries himself in liquor.and amphetamines ("What the shit did Elvis do except take dope that I couldn't git ahold of?" Lewis tells an interviewer after Elvis's death), he

145

smashes up cars, wastes his fortune, is accused by Myra Gale of beatings and torture, he shoots his bass player—two shots in the chest. In Goldman's *Elvis*, one is reading about human garbage; the premise is that there is nothing to understand, not in Presley's life and not in his music. *Hellfire* is driven by the need to understand—to understand what forces shaped music as powerful as "Whole Lotta Shakin' Goin' On," and to understand what shape those forces caused the man who made that music to take once he had made it—and it is driven by the need to make that understanding real to other people. So while in Tosches's book we are offered sins galore, there is not a titillating moment in its pages; while one can be happy one is not Jerry Lee Lewis—and the ending of *Hellfire* is as bleak and fearsome as one will read in a biography of a person not yet dead—one can never feel superior to him. Even so, empathy is not the test of biography, implication is. Anyone who ever said yes to "Whole Lotta Shakin' Goin' On" will likely find a place in *Hellfire*. Why is it so much finer than any book on Elvis Presley? Perhaps only because a particular writer was more interested in Lewis than in Elvis, in freedom than in slavery.

1986–1990

Emanations, Sightings, Disappearances, or a Seance of Eighteen Mediums

Spring 1986. Margaret Atwood, *The Handmaid's Tale.* Not long into the future, when the U.S.A. has become the Republic of Gilead, a theocracy that has replaced the Constitution with the Bible, a slave sings forbidden music to herself: "I feel so lonely, baby/I feel so lonely, baby/I feel so lonely, I could die." She doesn't know where it came from.

8 January 1987. Larry Speakes, White House Press Briefing. Noting that he was born in Mississippi, he opened by playing a tape of "That's All Right (Mama)." He continued with the announcement that while he had no new information on the president, virtually in hiding since the onset of the Iran-contra scandal, reporters could ask him "anything at all about the King."

Summer 1987. Lucy de Barbin with Dary Matera, *Are You Lonesome Tonight? The Untold Story of Elvis Presley's One True Love—and the Child He Never Knew.* In a season dominated by dead rock stars, scheduled to peak on August 16 with the 10th Annual Graceland Wake 'n' Family Picnic, the true author of the moment may be not Elvis Presley but Roger Peterson—the moonlighting pilot who on 3 February 1959 took his single-engine Bonanza off the ground and almost immediately returned to it, along with Buddy Holly, the Big Bopper, and Ritchie Valens. If Elvis now seems buried beneath his own clichés, the plane crash is still turning up surprises.

147

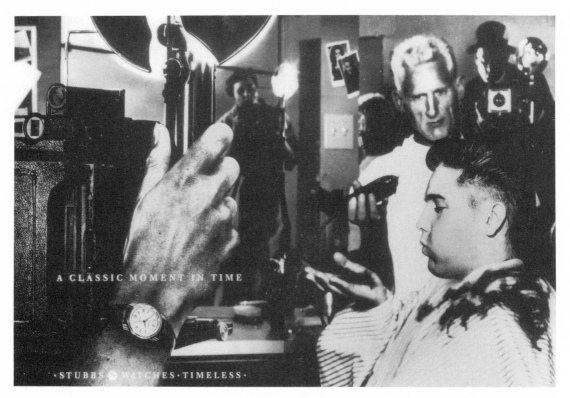

A CLASSIC MOMENT IN TIME

·STUBBS WATCHES·TIMELESS·

Advertisement for Stubbs Watches, U.K., 1989.

Not that the plane crash has failed to generate its own clichés, most of them regarding the saintliness of those who died young and, unlike Elvis, left more or less good-looking corpses, or anyway unconflicted memories of same. Thus Luis Valdez's hit film *La Bamba* is a straight Hollywood version of The Ritchie Valens Story, a heart-tugging exercise in melodramatic foreshadowing redeemed only by Danielle von Zernick's sunny performance as Valens's real-life girlfriend Donna Ludwig and Marshall Crenshaw's sly portrayal of Holly as a hipster on his way to turning into a beatnik; thus Los Lobos's lifeless folkie soundtrack covers of Valens tunes are flooding the airwaves (*their* "La Bamba" is number one; Valens's only made the top twenty). That is why Jim Dodge's *Not Fade Away* is a shock. Despite taking its title from a Holly song, this is The Big Bopper Story—a novel based in gnomic moments no biography will ever reach.

In San Francisco, in 1965, a young ex-trucker named George Gastin is hanging on to what's left of the Beat scene, making his rent smashing up expensive cars so their owners can collect on inflated insurance policies. Then his life starts to fall apart, and he loses his nerve, or finds it: handed a cherry '59 Cadillac a client wants torched, Gastin hesitates. In the glove compartment, he discovers an unmailed letter from the original owner, a wealthy spinster three years dead. "I am a 57-year-old virgin," it begins. "I've never had sex with a man because none has ever moved me." But the man to whom the letter is addressed moved her. One night, dialing for a classical station, the woman chanced upon "Chantilly Lace" and had her life changed. The Cadillac, the letter says, is her way of returning the gift: it's meant for the man on the radio, the Big Bopper himself. But the letter is dated 1 February 1959. Along with every rock 'n' roll fan in America, the woman heard the news.

Gastin determines to take the car where it belongs, heading for the Big Bopper's grave in Texas, then swerving north toward Clear Lake, Iowa, site of the plane crash, where the spinster's hero is symbolically, truly buried. Along the way Gastin moves through a series of haphazard, ultimately mystical encounters with phantom characters as odd and believable as the virgin fan of "Chantilly Lace": a mad scientist testing theories that later showed up in Jacques Attali's *Noise*, the world's greatest traveling salesman, the ninety-seven-year-old woman who owns the land where the plane went down, all of them from the same vein in American fiction first mined by Melville in *The Confidence-Man*. What drives *Not Fade Away* is Gastin's growing suspicion that he is destined to join this spectral company—to lose his status as a man with a place in time and become a road spirit, fading out as surely as a song heard on a car radio in the middle of the Nevada desert, or on a fine walnut console in a rich woman's house in San Francisco.

Still, in a publisher's summer glutted by such 10th Annual corpse-in-your-mouth product as Jane and Michael Stern's sneering *Elvis World* (complete with fake gilt jacket—the stuff looks like it'd flake off on your fingers, and that's the point), Lucy de

149

Cover and news report from the *Sun* (U.S.), 20 September 1988.

150

Barbin's memoir supersedes Jim Dodge's tale—not in the annals of rock, but in the annals of psychopathology. That is, de Barbin claims to remember every detail of her more than two-decade love affair with Elvis, an affair that long preceded and outlasted Elvis's marriage to Priscilla, and which resulted in two pregnancies and one child (who, out of respect for Elvis's public position, de Barbin never mentioned to him), and I believe she does remember. One day, a woman heard a song on the radio, and it sparked a fantasy, shared by millions, that the singer was singing directly to her. Rather than accept the cruelty and degradation of her real life, unlike the rest who heard the song the woman lived out the fantasy, and she is living it out today. In other words, the same radio that in *Not Fade Away* made a lonely woman happy made Lucy de Barbin pregnant.

Spring 1988.   Joni Mabe, *Love Letter to Elvis*, Primitivo Gallery, San Francisco. The exhibition was called "Elvis the King, a Folk Hero"; amidst Howard Finster's dubious tramp-art tributes and various imitations of Guy Peellaert's 1973 *Rock Dreams* paintings, Mabe's rough collages made noise. With *Elvis Tours Central America, Brings Hope to Hopeless, Food to the Hungry*, two Elvises in Army fatigues rose over the subcontinent like Sgt. York Godheads; with *Love Letter*, a giant, handwritten valentine, you couldn't tell the dementia from the parody, if there was any. Reading along with "You could have discovered that sex and religion could be brought together in your feelings for me," you were pulled up short by the closing "Confession": "I'm carrying your child. The last Elvis imitator I fucked was carrying your sacred seed. Please send money. Enclosed are photographs of myself and the earthly messenger you sent." In the middle of the collage there was a photo of a huge, ugly, ceramic Elvis-doll head; all around the border were snapshots of Mabe rubbing her bare breasts against the object, grinning.

Fall 1988.   Pet Shop Boys, "Always on My Mind," from *Intro-spection*. A nine-minute remake of their worldwide smash shorter

Maiden Jest, Inc., greeting card, 1985.

remake of the 1972 Elvis hit—done precisely as Elvis would have done it in Las Vegas, as a heart-tugging lament for his lost wife, a saddened mea culpa, the orchestra sawing away here as there, the female chorus washing up through the strings. Everything is in place, except for the disruptions of the drum machine and the wrong singer, who for a spoken passage has his already thin voice twisted up to near-Chipmunks level, then down to 16 rpm, only to come back as a human being, full of bile, bent on the revenge in the song Elvis must have felt constrained to leave out. As sung by a former rock journalist, it's a new kind of record: rock 'n' roll that writes its own history, corrects its own past, and contains its own criticism.

December 1988. McKenzie Wark, "Elvis: Listen to the Loss," *Art & Text* #31. As mediated through Walter Benjamin's "The Work of Art in the Age of Mechanical Reproduction," a revival of the classic theme of the king's two bodies—one his own, flesh and mortal, the other public and divine: "Like all temporal Kings who take their power seriously, Elvis felt the tug of a higher power he couldn't name. He sought the key to his immaterial power in books of occult lore and charismatic christian prophecy, but without success. For it was a power more quotidian and quixotic than any hand-me-down mysticism could describe. It was, of course, the modern power of recording, piling up rhythm & images & sounds & stories like so many bones of the body of Elvis, laying them up until they piled high into the air. A massive legacy of cliché quotation & anecdote & moral fable, soaring up high and solid as a rock—but also spinning outward, proliferating out of control. Till the time came when Elvis himself became a mere corporeal appendage to a great body of recording. A corpus so monstrous and obscene as to make his actual body seem sane and straight by comparison.

"Elvis made his famous last stand in the 1968 television show. He took back his earliest borrowings; his bluesy meanness, his black leather skins. He reclaimed what he had already borrowed. He hit out against the power of his own image, a final attempt to live up to a vast immaterial body by steeling himself, losing weight, drying out, honing his chops. He became what he beheld. This concert was a doomed attempt to recreate the presence of the original rock 'n' roll performance, to 'retake' all that was lost back into the body and make it whole again.

"But it was too late. The television cameras took care of that. Every spark of corporeal presence was captured and recorded. After the concert this fine recording was held against him, and inevitably he failed to measure up. Nothing was left but for the last embarrassing traces of Elvis to wither and die, and his bones laid to rest in the dust. Recording washed its hands of Elvis, and put the pressing plants on double shift."

24 January 1989. David Feldman, "Lucky Strike News Caravan," on the Alex Bennett Show, KITS-FM, San Francisco. Dramatic newsbreak music up, then rising sound of tickertape: "Three weeks of *extensive investigation* have uncovered a dramatic answer to the riddle, 'WHO MURDERED J.F.K.?' There's a *sensational*

153

link between the death of Elvis Presley and that of the president. Elvis was murdered by *assassins* who wanted to create a crackpot network of people who believed that he was still alive. Why? Because then the people who think Elvis is still alive would make Kennedy conspiracy buffs look like crackpots, too. Any new evidence suggesting that Lee Harvey Oswald didn't act alone could be belittled with, 'Oh yeah. And Elvis is working in a Burger King in Fremont. *Right.*' And there are *astonishing similarities* between the death of Elvis and the death of the president. Elvis died on the toilet. Kennedy died in *Dallas*. Kennedy had a secretary named 'Lincoln.' Presley's manager was named 'Colonel.' There were 'colonels' during the Civil War—a war run by 'Lincoln.' Kennedy died in 1963: Presley in 1977. Both numbers have *four digits*. Ed Sullivan shot Elvis from the waist up. Kennedy was shot from the *head down*. Presley slept with Priscilla Presley. *Kennedy* slept with Priscilla Presley . . ."

February 1989. Roy Orbison, interview with Nick Kent, *The Face*. "I first saw Elvis live in '54. It was at the Big D Jamboree in Dallas and first thing, he came out and spit on the stage . . . it affected me exactly the same way as when I first saw that David Lynch film. I didn't know what to make of it. There was just no reference point in the culture to compare it."

1989. Mekons, "Memphis, Egypt," from *"The Mekons Rock 'n' Roll"*. "A new religion," Alannah Myles sings of Elvisism in her hit "Black Velvet"; the Mekons' Elvis paintings on the covers of this disc are militantly anti–black velvet, unfixed and unclear, almost in motion. The faces peer out from under layers of cultural grime, hardly recognizable unless you know what to look for (the back portrait is so crepuscular it might as well be a photo of the Shroud of Memphis). They say that as rock epistemology "Memphis, Egypt" must be more than a correction of Talking Heads' "Cities," where David Byrne sang so passionately of "Memphis—home of Elvis, and the ancient Greeks." As an account of the twelve-year-struggle of one band of Leeds outsiders not "to be consumed by rock 'n' roll," the song like the pictures hints at

154

some final, irreducible exile not only from but in the home of rock 'n' roll—but the music does not make it past vanity. The suggestiveness remains in the paintings, and even they may not stand up to the work of Donald Paterson of Oakland, California. He is a mentally disabled artist with a vocabulary of twelve words; his "Elvis in Egypt" is a dense, gorgeous tapestry, a wall hanging or a floor rug, that shows the Memphis Flash cruising the pyramids in a pink Cadillac, stopping to pick up a hitchhiker.

Fall 1989. Michael Barson, *Rip It Up!—Postcards from the Heyday of Rock 'n' Roll.* Made out of forgotten movie posters, sheet music, concert programs, and fan magazines, notably the now hard to credit *Tommy Sands vs. Belafonte and Elvis.* Barson's caption on the message side of the card: "Sands had one fairly huge hit early in 1957, 'Teen-Age Crush,' and never saw the Top Ten again, though he did marry Nancy Sinatra. Brooklyn-born Harry Belafonte fared better, with several calypso-flavored hits in 1956 and '57, and a long life as an LP artist who appealed to an older audience. Elvis had a few hits, was drafted, then returned to driving a truck for Crown Electric in Memphis and was never heard from again."

11 August 1990. Dennis Leary, interview with James Brown, *New Musical Express.* "It's a good thing Jesus died when he did," says the stand-up comedian, "because if he hadn't, he'd have ended up like Elvis—he already had his disciples who were the equivalent of the Memphis Mafia. You don't want to be 42 years old and wearing diapers in your mansion—part of the fun of enjoying fame and fortune is that you can move your bowels almost at will . . ." The true strangeness of these seemingly banal lines— which crop up in almost identical form in the routines of any number of nightclub comics—may be no more than a matter of the confusion of its syntax and tenses, in the bottomless subjectivity of the English language, but revelation is where you find it: here, in one of the hundreds of jokes gleaned from *Elvis: What Happened?* and Albert Goldman's biography, is the most absolute and

155

uncanny of all the identifications of Elvis and Jesus. Elvis is presented as Jesus's precursor—not as his reflection, or even as his reembodiment. Jesus is not Elvis's avatar: Elvis is *his*.

28 August 1990. James Ledbetter, "Media Blitz," *Village Voice*. "There are weeks when it feels like *New York* magazine exists solely to pander to white fear and ignorance: check out the August 20 issue, in which Edwin Diamond dissects 'reverse reality' in the black media. In a paragraph on black conspiracy theories, Diamond asserts that 'no idea is too farfetched if it can be traced to white racism.' As an example, he cites the fact that WILB radio host Gary Byrd went to Nairobi because 'African doctors may have developed a cure for AIDS, and as the *Amsterdam News* reported, Byrd and the African-American community want to "claim the discovery before others discount the research as inconclusive or non-African." ' Diamond treats this as so self-evidently absurd he doesn't bother to explain or comment; it's as if Byrd had argued that Elvis was black". . . . *1979.* Linda Ray Pratt, "Elvis, or the Ironies of a Southern Identity." ". . . Elvis was truly different, in all those tacky Southern ways one is supposed to rise above with money and sophistication. . . . His taste never improved, and he never recanted anything. He was the sharecropper's son in the big house, and it always showed. Compounding his case was the fact that Elvis didn't always appear fully white. Not sounding white was his first problem, and white radio stations were initially reluctant to play his records. Not to be clearly white was dangerous because it undermined the black-white rigidities of a segregated society, and to blur those definitions was to reveal the falseness at the core of segregation. Racial ambiguity is both the internal moral condemnation and the social destruction of a racist society which can only justify itself by abiding by its own taboos. Yet all Southerners know, despite the sternest Jim Crow laws, that more than two hundred years of racial mixing has left many a Southerner racially ambiguous. White Southerners admit only the reality of blacks who have some white blood, but, of course, the knife cuts both ways. Joe Christmas and Charles Bon. Desirée's Baby. In most pictures, Elvis might resemble a blue-eyed Adonis, but in some of those early black and white photographs, his eyes sultry, nostrils flared, lips sullen, he looked just that—black and white". . . . *Summer 1990.* Ben Vaughn, "In the Presence of Legends: Charlie Feathers," *The Bob* #39. ". . . the subject turns to Elvis and Charlie closes the door, darts his eyes around the room, and whispers to us . . . 'Not too many people know it, but Gladys took a trip to Florida without Vernon and was carryin' on with a colored fella down there and was pregnant right after. Nope, Vernon ain't his daddy. No sir.' "

From left, unidentified man, Nappy Brown, Junior Parker, Elvis Presley, and Bobby Bland, Memphis, about 1956. Photo by E. C. Withers, Steve LaVere Collection, courtesy Michael Ochs Archives.

Fall 1990. Anonymous sex solicitation ad.

1990. Edwin S. Leek, "My Happiness," from Elvis Presley, *The Great Performances*. If you were watching ABC's *Elvis* series on February 6, you saw its Elvis, Michael St. Gerard, mime "My Happiness," originally a 1948 hit for the Pied Pipers (the voice belonged to veteran Elvis imitator Ronnie McDowell). You saw an eighteen-year-old enter Sam Phillips's "Memphis Recording Service" (pay two bucks, make a record) to sing a song for his mother's birthday: so the legend has said since 1956. But because Elvis made this recording—his first of any kind—in June 1953, and Gladys Presley's birthday fell in April, it was concluded long ago that Elvis cut the record for himself, to hear his own voice, hoping someone would notice. Someone did: the late Marion Keisker, Sun's co-manager, taped part of the performance for Phillips. "Good ballad singer," she wrote on the box.

For more than three decades all traces of the music were believed lost; the real thing—the one-copy, 78 rpm acetate disc—turned up some years ago in the possession of Elvis's high-school friend Edwin Leek. He claimed Elvis brought it to his house so he could hear his own voice (Leek had a record player, the Presleys didn't), and forgot to take it home; having been authenticated by Phillips and Keisker, it has been duly released as the lead track on the by-now traditional random assemblage of Elvis hits and standards. And it carries a further reversal: despite Leek's prosaic, perfectly

158

believable account, the two minutes and thirty-three seconds of music sing the old story. The performance is the purest distillation of devotion imaginable; it is almost impossible to believe it is not meant for a single, beloved listener, very hard to hear it as part of a career, or even as a wish for one. Yet at the same time the piece is intensely crafted, careful and precise, fully realized nineteenth-century parlor music, a work of art: the last, suspended moment, one can think, before the beginning of the present age. The teenager slides his voice over the sentimental lyric, slips down below the quiet melody, then almost imperceptibly rises beyond it, and the listener to whom the music must have been addressed vanishes, in her place a constructed, willed version of a single, unique individual. "Who do you sing like?" Marion Keisker asked Elvis that day. "I don't sing like nobody," he said, and the recording proves he was already right.

The release of this music, though, has passed unnoticed. Its charm has not gotten it played on the radio and its historical status has not gotten it written about. For all but a few it has disappeared once again. Which is to say that in the face of the diffusion of Elvis as a myth, the concentration of Elvis Presley as a person who once did interesting things has become irrelevant; that up against the perversity and complexity of Elvis's myth, its infinite circularity, capable of turning any merely human attribute into a phantasm, Elvis Presley's physical presence in a song is redundant above all.

1990

A Corpse in Your Mouth: Adventures of a Metaphor, or Modern Cannibalism

People who talk about revolution and class struggle without referring explicitly to everyday life, without understanding what is subversive about love and positive in the refusal of constraint, have corpses in their mouths. —Raoul Vaneigem, Paris, 1967.

The slaughter increases, and [people] cling to the prestige of European glory . . . they cannot persuade us to enjoy this rotting pile of human flesh they present to us. —Hugo Ball, Switzerland, 1916.

"HURRAY, BUTTER IS EVERYTHING! Goering in his Hamburg address: 'Brass has always made an empire strong; butter and lard have at best made a people fat.'"

—John Heartfield, photocollage, Prague, 1935.

The only objective way of diagnosing the sickness of the healthy is by the incongruity between their rational existence and the possible course their lives might be given by reason. All the same, the traces of illness give them away: their skin seems covered by a rash printed in regular patterns, like a camouflage of the inorganic. The very people who burst with proofs of exuberant vitality could easily be taken for prepared corpses, from whom the news of their not-quite-successful decease has been withheld for reasons of population policy. —Theodor Adorno, U.S.A., 1944.

In an era when art is dead [the student] remains the most loyal patron of the theatres and film clubs and the most avid consumer of its preserved corpse . . .   —Association fédérative générale des étudiants de Strasbourg/Internationale situationniste, *De la misère en milieu étudiant* (On the Poverty of Student Life), Strasbourg, France, Fall 1966, as translated by the Situationist International in *Ten Days that Shook the University: The Situationists at Strasbourg*, London, early 1967.

People who talk about revolution and class struggle without referring explicitly to everyday life, without understanding what is subversive about love and positive in the refusal of constraint, have corpses in their mouths.
—Raoul Vaneigem, *Traité de savoir-vivre à l'usage des jeunes générations* (Treatise on Living for the Young Generations), Paris, Fall 1967.

People who talk about revolution and class struggle without . . .
—Wall poster, Comité Enragés-Internationale situationniste, Paris, May 1968.

PEOPLE WHO TALK ABOUT REVOLUTION AND CLASS STRUGGLE WITHOUT . . .   —Anonymous graffiti, Paris, May 1968.

ART IS DEAD—DON'T CONSUME ITS CORPSE

—Anonymous graffiti, Paris, May 1968.

People who talk about revolution and class struggle without . . .

—Various unauthorized translations of Vaneigem's *Treatise*, published in pirate editions as *The Revolution of Everyday Life*, U.S.A. and U.K., late 1960s–early 1970s.

People who talk about revolution and class struggle without . . .

—Translation of Comité Enrages-Internationale situationniste wall poster in *Leaving the 20th Century: The Incomplete Work of the Situationist International*, edited by Christopher Gray, designed by Jamie Reid, U.K., 1974.

—Jamie Reid, collage from *Leaving the 20th Century*.

It's like someone just told me there aren't going to be anymore cheeseburgers in the world.

—Felton Jarvis, record producer for Elvis Presley, on the occasion of Presley's death, U.S.A., August 1977.

PRESLEYBURGER SHOCK

Shock. Horror. They are the only two words to describe the latest report from our Pick of the Poseurs correspondent in America. The recently described sensational attempt to steal Elvis' body was doomed to failure from the start, reason being a successful snatch has already been staged.

probe the sicker this bizarre situation has turned out to be. It seems even more rare and more sought after 'Dean burger specials', made from the remains of James Dean can be bought. Those who have tasted this speciality said they are rather tough but tasty. They are thought to be authentic however, as they still contain bits of the car wreckage.

'Disneyburgers' are quite a diff-

Shock. Horror. They are the only two words to describe the latest report from our Pick of the Poseurs correspondent in America. The recently described sensational attempt to steal Elvis' body was doomed to failure from the start, reason being a successful snatch has already been staged. What's happened to the body? It now appears certain that it was minced down and turned into the most bizarre cult food of all time. Certainly 'Presleyburgers' have been selling to the New York and West Coast rock aristocracy at up to $1000 a throw. Unconfirmed reports suggest that a small consignment of frozen Presleyburgers have arrived in U.K. and that Cliff Richard ate one just before going on at his recent Dome gig.

P.O.T.P. reporters have questioned rock superstar Frankie

Vaughn and though he declined to reply, his mouth was clearly seen to water. P.O.T.P. readers can draw their own conclusions.

The further we went with our probe the sicker this bizarre situation has turned out to be. It seems even more rare and more sought after 'Death Burger Specials,' made from the remains of James Dean can be bought. Those who have tasted this specialty said they are rather tough but tasty. They are thought to be authentic however, as they still contain bits of the car wreckage.

'Disneyburgers' are quite a different matter however, as they had the good sense to deep freeze him only twenty minutes after he had died. Walt Disney will have quite a surprise however when they wake him up in the year 2,000 AD and finds a couple of his arms and legs missing. —Anonymous text (by Ray Holme and Joby Hooligan) in *Pic of the Poseurs—Magazine for Modern Youth*, London, 1977.

—Jamie Reid, back sleeve of Sex Pistols single "Satellite" (B-side of "Holidays in the Sun"), London, Fall 1977.

—TC + P/Hipgnosis, front sleeve of Cortinas single "Defiant Pose," London, 1978.

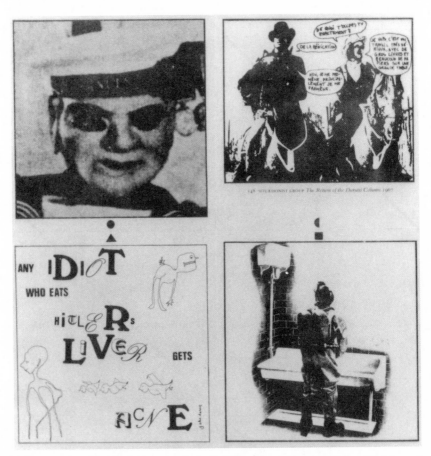

—Stickers enclosed with *A Factory Sample*, EP with recordings by Joy Division, the Durutti Column, John Dowie, and Cabaret Voltaire, 1978.

166

—Sleeve of Siouxsie and the Banshees single "Mittageisen—for John Heartfield" ("pluck cogs from fob watches / for dinner on Friday"), London, 1979.

—Jamie Reid, front sleeve of Sex Pistols single
"C'mon Everybody," featuring the late Sid
Vicious, London, 1979.

—Jamie Reid, rough design for sleeve of "C'mon Everybody." "The idea of the Vicious-Burger related back to the spoof we did as the Wicked Messengers. When Presley's body was lying in state at Graceland, there were loads of rumours about people trying to break in and steal it. We invented this little campaign—in a spoof fanzine called *Pick of the Poseurs*—saying that in fact his body had been stolen and had been turned into a commercial product—i.e., hamburgers. It also related to the old Situationist 'corpse' metaphor." —Jamie Reid, in *Up They Rise: The Incomplete Works of Jamie Reid*.

... the King's decaying body is exhumed and brought back for one last concert tour (unfortunately, it keeps falling off its stool and collapsing onstage in a heap). The corpse is trotted out for record-store autographing sessions. . . . Finally, slices of flesh are hacked off and sold in "Piece o' Presley" packages.

—*Rolling Stone*, on John Myhre's film *He May Be Dead, But He's Still Elvis*, U.S.A., 1979.

OUR FOREIGN CORRESPONDENT WRITES:

Top show biz moguls and TV personalities were convicted last week of eating Viciousburgers at New York's prestigious Studio 54 Disco, after the latest of a series of Vice Squad raids on the "playground of the idle rich."

Virgin Record Company boss, Richard Branson, 37, TV personality Dick Clark, 55, David Frost, 42, and several journalists, including Michael Watts, 38, editor of a music paper, were seen consuming several burgers each in what has been described as an "orgy of vampirism." "It was horrific," said clubgoer Richard DeNunzio of Brooklyn, "They each had several corpses in their mouths." More showbiz and media names, including some well-known News Reporters, are expected to be convicted as the hearings continue.

The last few years have seen an increase in this bizarre cult of vampirism, of which the Viciousburger is only the latest example. Vampires are noteworthy for consuming star corpses in the form of burgers in the mistaken belief that some of the star's charisma will rub off on them; sadly, as you can see, these attempts are doomed to failure and these cultists deluded. The cult is said to have begun in the 50's with Deanburgers; these were very rare, and contained bits of Porsche wreckage and sunglasses—those cultists still alive who tasted them say "They were tough but tasty." Perhaps the worst outbreak of vampirism before the Viciousburger scandal was the Presleyburger scandal of 1977. The scandal was discovered when an attempt was made to steal Presley's body from the grave by occultists: the body was already stolen! It now appears

169

that it was minced down and turned into the bizarre cult food, Presleyburgers. These are said to be very expensive ($1000 a throw) and high on fatty content, but it still didn't deter the thrill-seeking showbiz crowd: Mick Jagger was said to have eaten several before his recent Wembly concert. Heavy prison sentences imposed in Canada on Keith Richard, another vampire, stopped the spread of this disgusting cult, but with the present Viciousburger scandals it seems to be flourishing. And even now, there are unconfirmed reports of Curtisburgers, grisly burgers with hints of rope and marble. There is no truth, however, in the rumour Hitlerburgers are freely available: they were only available post-war and reserved for VIP's.

—Anonymous text (by Jon Savage) found among the Jamie Reid Collection acquired by the Victoria and Albert Museum, London, 1979.

. . . there was even talk of having Elvis's corpse dug up and the stomach analyzed for traces of drugs which led me to fantasize: Can you imagine anything more thrilling than getting to stick your hand and forearm through the hole in Elvis's rotted guts slopping whatever's left of 'em all over each other getting the intestinal tracts mixed up with the stomach lining mixed up with the kidneys as you forage fishing for incriminating pillchips sufficient to slap this poor sweating doctor 20,000 years in Sing Sing and add one more hot clip to Geraldo's brochure of heroically humanitarian deeds done entirely in the interests of bringing the public the TRUTH it has a constitutional right to know down to the last emetic detail which they in time get as you pull your arm out of dead Elvis's innards triumphantly clenching some crumbs off a few Percodans, Quaaludes, Desoxyns, etc. etc. etc. and then once off camera now here's where the real kick to end 'em all comes as you pop those little bits of crumbled pills in your own mouth and swallow 'em and get high on drugs that not only has Elvis Presley himself also gotten high on the exact same not brand but the pills themselves they've been laying up there inside him per-

170

haps even aging like fine wine plus of course they're all slimy with
little bits of the disintegrating insides of Elvis's pelvis

SO YOU'VE ACTUALLY GOTTEN TO *EAT* THE
KING OF ROCK 'N' ROLL!

which would be the living end in terms of souvenirs, fetishism,
psychofandom, the collector's mentality, or even just hero-worship
in general. Notice I am leaving out such pursuits as necrophilia
and coprophagy—there are admittedly some rather delicate dis-
tinctions to be made here, some fine lines to be drawn, but to those
so insensitive as not to perceive them I will simply say that calling
this act something like "necrophilia" would be in poor taste and
if there was one thing Elvis always stood for it was good taste and
maintaining the highest standards that money could buy so fuck
you, you're just jealous, go dig up Sid Vicious and eat him, but
if you do please save some for me because I'd like if possible just
a small say 3″ × 3″ hunk out of his flank because what I want to
do is eat the flesh under the skin, then dry the epidermis itself
which isn't all that tasty anyway and slip it in the sleeve of my
copy of *Sid Sings* as a souvenir to show my grandchildren and
perhaps take out and wrap around my dick every once in a while
when I'm masturbating cause a little more friction always helps
get the wank achieved and sometimes I have found that when I
literally can't get it up to jerk off because I'm too alienated from
everything including my own cock if I take a scrap of dried skin
from a dead rockstar—trade you an Al Wilson in mint condition
well as mint as dead can be anyway for a Jim Morrison I don't
care how shot to shit—it really seems to do the trick.

But I digress. Jerking off with some of Sid's track-riddled forearm could not even be called child's play compared to the exquisite
sensation of eating those pills and gore out of Elvis. I mean, I read
Terry Southern's "The Blood of a Wig" too, but that was written
before the age of the celebrity, as Marisa Berenson told *People*
magazine when they put her on the cover: "My ambition is to
become a saint." *My* ambition is to become a parasite on saints,
which shouldn't be too difficult, I mean they're supposed to get

171

holier through physical mortification and all that, right? Plus I know about how Idi Amin used to dine on the flesh and drink the blood of his onetime enemies while lecturing their severed heads in a line on the desk in his office concerning the improprieties they committed while alive so I don't need to go get *The Golden Bough* just to prove to everybody else what I already know because it's simple horse sense which is if I eat a little bit of Elvis (the host, as it were, or is that mixing mythologic metaphors?) then I take on certain qualities possessed by Elvis while he was alive and walking around or laying in bed with the covers over his head as the case may be, and when these pills make me high they'll put me on the Elvis trip to end 'em all as I'll be seeing what he saw and thinking what he thought perhaps up to the last final seconds before kicking the bucket and if all of this works well enough as it most certainly will I intend to be greedy when offered the chance of a lifetime and scoop out a whole giant rotten glob of his carcass that let's face it he's never gonna need again and I eat from deep in the heart of him as I fully intend to do, why, THEN I WILL BE ELVIS! I'll make several dozen unwatchable movies and that number plus a couple dozen more unlistenable albums! I'll know karate so I can kick out the eyeballs of my landlord next time he comes up here to complain I haven't paid the rent in three months! Like I'm sure he's gonna come complaining to Elvis about something as piddling as rent anyway! Ditto for Master Charge, Macy's, all these assholes hounding me for money I don't have and they don't need: I mean, seriously, can you imagine *Elvis* sitting down with his checkbook and a stack of unpaid bills, going through the whole dreary monthly routine, and then balancing his bank account? He'd just go out and buy a car for some colored cleaning lady he'd never met before instead! Then Master Charge would tear up the bill saying "Mr. Presley you are a real humanitarian and since we are too we want to say we feel honored to have you run up as high a tab as you want on us."

Lessee, now, what else can I do? Well, concerts. Kinda boring, tho, since all I've gotta do (all I'm ALLOWED to do if I'm gonna not insult Elvis's memory by breaking with tradition) is just stand there holding a microphone, singing current schmaltz with no emotion, and occasionally wiping the sweat off my brow with one of a series of hankies hidden away in the sleeve of my White Castle studded jacket and then toss the contaminated little rag to whichever female in the first few rows has walked more backs, blackened more eyes and broken more arms and legs in attempt to get up close to my godly presence. As my whole career has surely borne out, I believe with one hand on my mother's grave that aggressive persistence in the service of a noble cause should be rewarded. Still, all this, ah, don't *you* think it sounds kinda, well, *dull?* I mean, how many hankies can you throw out before you start to go catatonic? At least Sid Vicious got to walk onstage with "GIMME A FIX" written in blood on his chest and bash people in the first row over the head with his bass if he didn't approve of the brand of beercan they were throwing at him.

Sid got to have all the fun.

> —Lester Bangs, "Notes for Review of Peter Guralnick's *Lost Highway*, 1980," published in Lester Bangs, *Psychotic Reactions and Carburetor Dung*, U.S.A., 1987.

The words in this pamphlet are not set out in the order in which they appear on the record, instead I have laid them out in the 3 groups in which I conceived them.

    (1) 6 corpses in the mouths of the Bourgoisie
    (2) 4 songs
    (3) ALBION, AWAKE!

> —Notes by Chris Cutler in booklet of lyrics enclosed with Art Bears LP *The World As It Is Today*, U.K., 1981.

—Page on Lennonburger in "This Could Happen to *Your* City! The Northern California Underground Uprising of '82," booklet included in anthology LP *Maximum Rock n Roll Presents Not So Quiet on the Western Front*, San Francisco, 1982.

Well, that's my story—and I'm stickin to that. So let's have another drink and—let's talk about the blues.

Blues is about *dignity*. It's about self-respect, and no matter what they take away from you, that's yours for keeps. I remember how it was, how every medium, TV and papers and radio and all those people were saying, "You're on the scrapheap, you're *useless*," and I remember how easy it was to start believin that, and I remember how you'd hear people *take it for granted* that it was true, just because someone with ah, an *ounce* of power said so. That's a problem now: too many oddballs, *pocket-book* sociologists and would-be philosophers with an axe to grind—but there's a solution! It's not easy; it's a matter of comin to terms in your *heart* with the situation you're in, and not havin things *forced* upon you. There're plenty of forces against you, forcing you against your will and your ideals. You've got to hope for the best—and that's the best you can hope for. It's hope against hope. I remember something Sal Paradise said. He said, "The city intellectuals of the world are *divorced* from the folk bloody body of the land and are just rootless fools!" So listen—when the smile, the condescending pat on the back comes and says, "We're sorry, but you're nothing, you've got nothing for us and we've got nothing for you"—you say, *no*, and say it loud, NO! Remember: People who talk about revolution and class struggle without referrin *explicitly* to everyday life, without understanding what is *subversive* about love and positive in the refusal of constraints—such people have a *corpse* in their *mouth*.　　　—Pete Wylie/Wah!, "The Story of the Blues, Part One and Part Two," U.K., 1982.

Dr. Allen Nadler reports that Chico has yet another claim to the title of culinary capital of the West: La Salle's, a great hangout, is now featuring the Belushi Burger—"Sloppy But Good."
　　　—Herb Caen, *San Francisco Chronicle*, 1982.

TRY OUR NEW KING-SIZE
ELVISBURGERS
WITH
CODEINE
MORPHINE
VALIUM
NEMBUTAL
PHENOBARBITAL
QUAALUDE
and 100% BEEF

—Ray Lowry, cartoon, London, 1983.　　175

Pop is a frustration machine. And one of its most interesting mechanisms is the tension between the star's incitement of desire and passion (not to mention hysteria) and the bureaucratic and ideological apparatus erected to protect stars from the consequences of this incitement.

At one point we interview Adam Ant's manager, Don Murfet, an expert in personal security. . . . Don turned out to be a wise and benevolent man, as genuinely concerned for the well-being of fans as stars. One month after this interview, his protégé Adam Ant appears on the front cover of *Sounds*, glowering lustily at all and sundry with both hands tucked into gaping flies. What was a fan to think?

It is hardly surprising, when stars offer themselves so lavishly for *consumption*, that some fans will take the invitation literally.

Like Mark Chapman.

After all, the only plausible way to "consume" people is to annihilate them. —Fred and Judy Vermorel, *Starlust: The Secret Fantasies of Fans*, London, 1985.

Burger King can't be getting over on the food, it must be the artwork. Burger King does what the Comte de Lautréamont and his surrealist followers only dreamed about. It creates a decadence you can taste.

Burger King sells the whole world the same democratic hamburger and to each burger buyer they say, "Have it your way" . . . And the hamburger is the most symbolic of foods. It is round, like the body of Christ in the Mass, but it's also hot and juicy. Like Frankenstein, it is a body made of many bodies. —Glenn O'Brien, *Artforum*, U.S.A., April 1986.

Sable sauntered in to the Burger Lord. It was exactly like every other Burger Lord in America. McLordy the Clown danced in the Kiddie Korner. The serving staff had identical gleaming smiles that never reached their eyes. And behind the counter a chubby, middle-aged man in a Burger Lord uniform slapped burgers onto the griddle, whistling softly, happy in his work.

Sable went up to the counter.

"Hello-my-name-is-Marie," said the girl behind the counter. "How-can-I-help-you?"

"A double blaster thunder biggun, extra fries, hold the mustard," he said.

"Anything-to-drink?"

"A special thick whippy chocobanana shake."

She pressed the little pictogram squares on her till. (Literacy was no longer a requirement for employment in these restaurants. Smiling was.) Then she turned to the chubby man behind the counter.

"DBTB, E F, hold mustard," she said. "Choc-shake."

"Uhnnhuhn," crooned the cook. He sorted the food into little paper containers, pausing only to brush the graying cowlick from his eyes.

"Here y'are," he said.

She took them without looking at him, and he returned cheerfully to his griddle, singing quietly, "Loooove me tender, looooove me long, neeever let me go . . ."

The man's humming, Sable noted, clashed with the Burger Lord background music, a tinny tape loop of the Burger Lord commercial jungle, and he made a mental note to have him fired.

—Neil Gaiman and Terry Pratchett, *Good Omens: The Nice and Accurate Prophecies of Agnes Nutter, Witch*, U.S.A., 1990.

A man dies and they want to serve him up for posterity. Serve him, so to speak, trussed up for our dear descendants at the table. So that they, napkin tucked under chin and armed with knife and fork, can dig in to the freshly deceased.

The deceased, as you know, have the inconvenient habit of cooling off too slowly, they're burning hot. So they are turned into aspics by pouring memories over them—the best form of gelatine.

177

And since deceased greats are also too large, they are cut down. The nose, they say, is served separately, or the tongue. You need less gelatine that way, too. And that's how you get yesterday's classic, a freshly cooked tongue-in-aspic. With a side dish of hoofs from the horse he used to ride.
—Blind fragment in untitled collage by Elvis Costello, 1989.

1990

Still Dead: Elvis Presley Without Music

The Last Temptation of Elvis: Songs from His Movies is a double album featuring twenty-six numbers by the likes of Bruce Springsteen ("Viva Las Vegas"), Tanita Tikaram ("Loving You"), the Primitives ("[You're So Square] Baby I Don't Care"), Dion DiMucci ("Mean Woman Blues"), the Blow Monkeys ("Follow That Dream"), Vivian Stanshall & the Big Boys ("[There's] No Room to Rhumba in a Sports Car"), the Reggae Philharmonic Orchestra ("Crawfish"), Nanci Griffith & the Blue Moon Orchestra ("Wooden Heart"), the Hollow Men ("Thanks to the Rolling Sea"—never heard of it), Sydney Youngblood (an acapella "[Let Me be Your] Teddy Bear"—never heard of him, but he's great), Les Negresses Vertes ("Marguerita"), Robert Plant ("Let's Have a Party"), and Pop Will Eat Itself ("Rock-a-Hula-Baby")—performers so disparate they can be called "the likes" only because of a common willingness to sing old Elvis songs.

This odd artifact—surprising on its own terms, aggressively inventive on anyone's, passionate, sarcastic, indecipherable and irony-free—is only one of countless bits of recent evidence attesting to Elvis Presley's refusal to go away. In fact, in 1990, a neat thirteen years after his death, a year lacking even an excuse for a major promotion organized around the silver or golden anniversary of something, Elvis appeared all over the map. Even people who insisted they could care less found it necessary to bring him up.

He did not appear, as in earlier years, in a supermarket in Kalamazoo, crossing a parking lot in Las Vegas, in the person of a long-lost unacknowledged child, or as a statue on Mars broadcasting "All Shook Up"—as confirmed by digital photographic simulations, tabloid weeklies (JESSE GARON ELVIS' PARASITIC TWIN?), hardcover bestsellers, and paperbacks packaged with cassettes of him calling from a pay phone. That story was already part of the myth, fixed and still, a mini-craze charted assiduously in "Bloom County" and "Doonesbury." Was Elvis living quietly in a furnished room over a bar in Flint, just a step away from the chained-up GM plant? K. I. Michasiw of York University in Ontario summed up the urban legend: "Elvis fakes his death and leads the common life he left to play through the desires of that common life. The transformation makes of Elvis a consumerist Tiresias, having had boundlessly he moves to a realm of dearth. And discovers . . . ? This consoling fantasy for the age of Reagan, of plant-closings and proletarianization, is not played out to answer that question. The way may be wretched but the King has chosen it too; he has given up his place amongst Reagan's rich and returned a chastened demigod to anonymity, to the impoverishing masses." Or, as Don Henley sang in "If Dirt Were Dollars": "I was flyin' back from Lubbock / I saw Jesus on the plane / Or maybe it was Elvis—you know they kinda look the same." "There's a very large spiritual gap in this country," Henley explained. "People are so hungry for a miracle, there've been more sightings of Jesus and Elvis than Bigfoot or the Loch Ness Monster."

But now Elvis appeared on the trickier terrain of art: every kind of art. Still enough like Jesus to get away with anything, as the titling of *The Last Temptation of Elvis* indicated, he sneaked out of the crevices of songs, movies, novels, comic strips, poems, scholarly works, and television shows, in a seemingly permanent ubiquity, most often moving like Manny Farber's "termite-tapeworm-fungus-moss art"—which, Farber wrote in 1962, "goes always forward eating its own boundaries," leaving "nothing in its path other than the signs of eager, industrious, unkempt activity."

He was not well dressed. In his thirteenth posthumous year Elvis Presley oozed from the fissures of culture, voracious and blind—blind to the glare cast by *Elvis*, the short-lived TV series that with exwife Priscilla as executive producer so vividly recreated his early

"Video Cassette Releases," *San Francisco Chronicle*, 18 November 1990.

years, by the *Life* cover proclaiming the "INESCAPABLE CONCLUSION" that he had killed himself, by the *Forbes* cover naming him the highest paid dead entertainer of the year—blind to the headlines and the money he could still make. This wasn't where he operated.

As Farber wrote, "the best examples of termite art" occur where "the spotlight of culture is nowhere in evidence," where "the craftsman can be ornery, wasteful, stubbornly self-involved, doing go-for-broke art and not caring what comes of it." A corpse doesn't care—and in the shape of Elvis, engorged and bleeding dope, the corpse is waste itself, but not still. Following the path of this termite, it's as if the present-day Elvis wants most of all to devour the culture that for so long has fed off of him.

I'm in heaven now
I can see you, Richard
Goodbye Hollywood
Goodbye Downey
Hello Janis
Hello Dennis
Elvis—
——Sonic Youth, "Tunic
(Song for Karen),"
1990.

Some folks up here look kind of surprised when they see I didn't go to The Other Place, the real warm place.

I say, why? I was good to my mommy and Priscilla, and, heck I did more gospel albums than most anybody else. Then they say, c'mon El, what about the movies?

——Liner notes to *The Last Temptation of Elvis*, 1990.

VILLAGE VOICE STRIKE BENEFIT: Galaxie 500, Mofungo, Frank's Museum, Krave, Tuli Kupferberg, Elvis Presley, in support of the paper's workers, whose contract expires June 30. June 17, CBGB, 315 Bowery, 982–4052.
——*Village Voice*, 19 June 1990.

The sound of him chewing is quiet but insistent. It's the sound of a monstrous 1950s atom-bomb-mutation-film cricket moving steadily across a field of corn. In the cornfield there is a scarecrow, got up in bulging gold-lamé Las Vegas jumpsuit, bejeweled heavy-weight championship belt, and jet-black pompadour—or clothed in rockabilly zoot-suit drape, the hair as it was in Memphis in 1954: almost blond. As the big cricket Elvis climbs a trouser leg and nibbles away at himself, only to reappear in the rags of many costumes, Gregor Samsa in reverse, Cinderella after the clock struck but ready for Saturday night, a saturnalia you'd probably just as soon stay home for.

This is one of the many guises in which Elvis has reemerged. This is the Bad Elvis, not just the mad prisoner of the American dream dropping down dead from his Graceland toilet with an astrological sex manual about the Shroud of Turin slipping from his hand, but a killer.

He talks out of the side of his mouth, but so wildly the tongue goes right through the cheek, the bug chewing, then a hand coming out the other side, waving. You can hear him talk in *Bad Influence*, as psychopath Rob Lowe exits from straight-up James Spader's apartment after killing Spader's cute girlfriend Lisa Zane and dumping her body in the bedroom: "Elvis," Lowe sneers as he strolls out the door, "has left the building." You can watch him as Andrew Dice Clay, hulking fantasy of date rape in black leather, bidding for mainstream dollars in *The Adventures of Ford Fair-lane*, his hair swept up into Elvis's black pouf, starring with Pris-cilla Presley herself. You can see him as Nicolas Cage's singing killer in David Lynch's *Wild at Heart*, crooning "Love Me" from a nightclub floor and then cutting a drunk punk all to pieces; you can see him as Benjamin Horne, Richard Beymer's character in Lynch's TV series *Twin Peaks*, and here he's really oozing.

"It occurred to me last night around 10:58," a friend wrote as *Twin Peaks* was setting up for its first false climax, "that with his taste for drugs and kink, not to mention his status as latter-day Bigfoot, it seems obvious that Elvis is the answer to 'Who Killed Laura Palmer?'" The comment fed off the fantasy of Elvis as homicidal maniac—not a new fantasy. Television's first Bad Elvis, and the most complex, rose up in 1986 in Michael Mann's *Crime*

Story, set in Chicago and Las Vegas in the early 1960s: Anthony Denison's young mobster prince Ray Luca. Under his enormous, scary lift of hair, his already outdated sideburns the mark of a man who kept the faith, he was moody, unsure, self-hating, always hinting that he could have turned out differently: he solved every doubt with a massacre. But in the corners of the public imagination, Elvis had always kept company with mass murderers, redneck nihilists. In flashes he could seem indistinguishable from Charles Starkweather (who like Elvis worshipped James Dean), or Richard Speck (a fan of Chuck Berry, Bo Diddley, Muddy Waters, the real thing—Elvis was never *his* king, Speck said before being sentenced to 1200 years in prison for the murder of eight nurses). Now, though, the once-coded secret was out. "It was such a waste, some stupid person," George Harrison said early in 1990, thinking about John Lennon and Mark Chapman. "If John had been killed by Elvis, it would have at least had meaning!" But my friend's fantasy of Elvis and Laura was almost redundant; with *Twin Peaks* it was already part of the show.

It didn't matter who the killer was, at the close of the series' first run—the killer as provisionally designated, and subject to change. It was clear weeks before that Richard Beymer was in on the death: that he was there for the torture, the last gang-bang. As Romeo in 1961 in *West Side Story* he'd been a pseudo-Elvis—or not pseudo, since his Italianate Tony perfectly matched the Big E's version of "O Sole Mio," "It's Now or Never" (recorded for *The Last Temptation of Elvis* by Paul McCartney). Forgotten ever since, flogging Tony for decades in summer stock, Beymer was back as Twin Peaks' Slime King, criminal property developer, town-eater, termite queen, rising from the bed of his mistress clutching a small, airplane-bar-sized Elvis liquor bottle. "Going to give Little Elvis a shower," he says.

One was meant to recall that, according to Albert Goldman's *Elvis*, "Little Elvis" was what Elvis called his penis. One realized that this was merely one of the non sequiturs *Twin Peaks* routinely piled on its red herrings. But one could also understand that it was as a non sequitur that Elvis Presley now did much of his work—and that long after *Twin Peaks* has been forgotten, Elvis will still be busy, and fecund. That little Elvis bottle—presumably Benjamin Horne used it as a dildo, but what was in it? Whiskey? Sperm? Homunculi?*

I'm sick of hearing about Elvis. I don't understand why people talk about him as if he's still *here*. But I have a friend who has a shrine to Elvis in his bathroom. When you flush the toilet these lights light up. He's got Quaalude bottles in front of it.

> —Caller on phone-in show "Why Elvis?" ("This nightmare," another caller named the program), KALX-FM, Berkeley, 12 March 1990.

SPIKE LEE: You don't got no wing in your house dedicated to Elvis Presley, do you?

EDDIE MURPHY: I have a room with some Elvis pictures in it. I have a room with lots of pictures of Elvis. . . . You don't find him fascinating?

LEE: I wish he never died myself, so I wouldn't have to hear about him every single day.

MURPHY: You know what's interesting about Elvis? When he was getting ready to die, Elvis was broke, wearing big platforms and was like a joke in show business. It shows you how fucked up society is, 'cause in the movies they only want happy endings and shit. What happened is, when this man died, that was their happy ending. Elvis was their American dream, the poor boy that got rich and they hated him for it. And then he died and they turned him into this god form. And I think that's fascinating.

> —*Spin*, October 1990.

---

* "I'm afraid you projected a vivid fantasy upon the 'Little Elvis' scene in *Twin Peaks*. I spoke to the best authority (Richard Beymer) and the 'small, airplane-bar-sized Elvis liquor bottle' was neither decanter nor bottle, and contained nothing of whiskey, sperm, or homunculi. It was actually a doll stuffed with cotton from the King's belly button—the only kind of cotton he ever picked." —Joni Mabe, letter to GM, 2 November 1990.

Tabloids scream
Elvis seen at a shopping mall
That's the kind of talk
That makes my stomach crawl
Picture a zombie Elvis
In a tacky white jumpsuit
Just imagine a rotting Elvis
Shopping for fresh fruit
—Living Colour,
"Elvis Is Dead," 1990.

ALL-TIME FAVOURITE ELVIS MOVIE?
Tracy of the Primitives: "Burger King" (Elvis The Autopsy)—this is a
bootleg video. —Notes to *The Last Temptation of Elvis*, 1990.

Me and Elvis
Never worried about the cops
He flashed that badge he got from Nixon
Every time that we got stopped
—Human Radio, "Me and Elvis," 1990.

Bill Barminski, panel from *King of the
Pre Fab* (Bar-min-ski Comix), 1984.

He was very flamboyant. . . . But as I talked to him, I sensed that he was a very shy man. The flamboyance was covering up the junk. . . . He wanted to be an example to young people. And people say that because later on it was found that he had used drugs, that therefore he could not be a good example. They overlooked the fact that he never used illegal drugs. It was always drugs prescribed by his physician.

—Richard Nixon, "Presidential Forum"
(prerecorded answer to programmed question),
Nixon Library, July 1990.

Elvis for Everyone was a 1965 album and a Top Ten hit, mixing renditions of "Santa Lucia" and Hank Williams's "Your Cheating Heart" with covers of Lonnie Johnson's "Tomorrow Night" and Billy "The Kid" Emerson's "When It Rains, It Really Pours," two numbers by black singers Elvis recorded in 1955 for Sun Records in Memphis, here touched up with Hollywood overdubs to make them "for everyone." Such appropriations by Elvis—or such appropriations of Elvis—were the subtext of Living Colour's "Elvis is Dead," the hard no of a black rock 'n' roll band bent on smashing the same racial barriers Elvis once smashed, the same barriers that had reformed around him. The song drove Elvis back into his grave—a furious I-should-have-been-the-King rap by Little Richard bumped hegemonic cavils from Mick Jagger's white square as a chorus chanted "ELVIS IS DEAD" in a dozen languages—and then redeemed him: it wasn't his fault. "The pelvis of Elvis/Too dangerous for the masses/They cleaned him up and sent him to Vegas/Now the masses are his slave." But the story is so big Living Colour too are part of it. If they refuse to be the masses, they must join the everyone, or even more than that. "Elvis came to me and told me to write the lyrics," said guitarist Vernon Reid: he was only speaking for—not "the King," just the man, whoever he could have been.

Elvis for everyone—whether you wanted him or not—was the truth in 1990, but only an emptied image. The social fact was "Elvis Is Everywhere," a 1987 single by Mojo Nixon and Skid Roper. As a comedy record it was made more for the tabloids than

187

a beat (there was one fabulously non sequitous moment, positing Elvis in, or as, the Bermuda Triangle: "Elvis needs boats!" Nixon shouted. "Elvis needs boats!"), but it was right soon enough: dead on release, it was a hit three years later, when the times caught up with it. You couldn't escape—not even watching the 1990 National Football Conference title game, as a McDonald's commercial came on. Two preteen sisters rush home to see "him" on the *Ed Sullivan Show* (apparently McDonald's paid to use Sullivan's name, but not "his"); they're gaga with anticipation. The family gathers around the TV, but just as Ed introduces "him," the set goes dead.

"Must be a blackout," says Dad—so he takes the girls to McDonald's for their "first time," an amazingly blunt double-entendre. A voice-over by a now grown-up daughter acknowledges that she and her sister "missed out on part of rock 'n' roll history—somehow, that night, it didn't seem to matter so much." "So," says Mom, back in 1956, as the family leaves the golden arches, "wasn't that better than ol' what's his name?" "Years later," says the grown-up daughter, "we found out there wasn't a blackout—Dad had pulled the plug!" *So we shot him*, countless viewers other than myself must have mouthed in reply. Elvis was everywhere, and each mask was simply the thing the thing wore over its true face, which no one could see. What was stranger—Elvis on network TV as pornographic fetish object, or Nanci Griffith, on *The Last Temptation*, making "Wooden Heart," probably the thing's worst big record, sound wonderful?

MOLLY DODD: You know, I didn't even know you had a car and—what a car it is!
DAVY (39-year-old Molly's doorman, a poker-faced Irishman in his fifties): My Caddy's one of my pride and joys.
MOLLY: It doesn't seem quite you, though, Davy.
DAVY: I bought it from one of the king's bodyguards in '72.
MOLLY: The king?
DAVY (bored with her obtuseness): Elvis.

188   —*The Days and Nights of Molly Dodd*, 25 May 1990.

[In 1956, in Berlin, American and British servicemen and their German girlfriends listen to U.S. Armed Forces Network radio.] They favored Screamin' Jay Hawkins's "I Put a Spell on You," and "Tutti Frutti." It was the latter, sung by Little Richard at the outer limit of effort and joy, that started them jiving. Then it was "Long Tall Sally". . . . In April came a song that overwhelmed everybody, and that marked the beginning of the end of Leonard's Berlin days. It was no use at all for jiving. It spoke only of loneliness and despair. Its melody was all stealth, its gloom comically overstated. He loved it all, the forlorn, sidewalk tread of the bass, the harsh guitar, the sparse tinkle of a barroom piano, and most of all the tough, manly advice with which it concluded: "Now if your baby leaves you, and you've got a tale to tell, just take a walk down Lonely Street . . ." For a time AFN was playing "Heartbreak Hotel" every hour. The song's self-pity should have been hilarious. Instead, it made Leonard feel worldly, tragic, bigger somehow.

—Ian McEwan, *The Innocent*, 1990.

"Stop this motherfucking Limo," says the King,
And the Caddie, halting, raises fins of dust
Into a landscape made of creosote,
Lizards, dismembered tires. The King's been reading
Again—*Mind Over Matter: Yogic Texts*
On Spiritual Renewal by Doctor Krishna
Majunukta, A Guide on How to Tap the
Boundless Powers of the Ancients.

Bodyguards and hangers-on pile out.
His Highness, shades off, scans the east horizon.
"Boys, today I'm gonna show you somethin'
You can tell your grandchildren about."

He aims a finger at Nevada's only cloud.
"Lo! Behold! Now watch that fucker move!"

—David Wojahn, "Elvis Moving a Small Cloud: The Desert Near
  Las Vegas, 1976—after the painting by Susan Baker," *Mystery*
  Train, 1990.

What made the *Molly Dodd* scene interesting was the obviousness loaded into its displacement—the unmannered, uncapitalized way Davy the Doorman was able to say "the king," as if he were referring to, say, the son of King Zog I, the pretender to the throne of Albania, who happened to live in Molly's New York apartment building, the residents of which naturally called him "the king," to be nice. The scene plays smoothly, and when Elvis enters he's a shock; given Molly's tony aura, even a reference to him seems more foreign than Zog could ever be. Elvis enters noisily but sideways, as he does also in Ian McEwan's brittle novel *The Innocent*, where his soft steps are cut precisely to the beat of the song you couldn't jive to. He is much less foreign here, in Berlin in 1956, than he is in Molly Dodd's building; in Berlin he's a world spirit, in Molly's lobby just white trash. Unnamed in *The Innocent*, he is nevertheless fully present, as a threat, a dare: the nervous propriety of McEwan's syntax, catching the hesitant attempt of a virgin listener to rise to the challenge of a new music, and not failing, testify to that. In a few lines, McEwan shows how an unknown singer created an irreversible event, an event that even if it could be forgotten could never be taken back. That's what makes "Elvis Moving a Small Cloud" so pathetic—didn't he know how many *lives* he'd moved?

Scrutiny of such traces is a way to find out: it means following the trail of the termite as it feels "its way through walls of particularization, with no sign that the artist has any object in mind other than eating away the immediate boundaries of his art, and turning these boundaries into the conditions of the next achievement." That's how Elvis—or the common wish to know who he was and what he did—gets from a TV show to a novel to a poem.

Farber's idea of termite art versus "white elephant art" ("an expensive hunk of well-regulated area") is useful because it points away from the stage—the place where, in the years before he died, Elvis Presley finally appeared exactly as a white elephant, so vividly that the metaphor, had one chosen to apply it, would no longer have been a metaphor. No new answers or for that matter any new questions will be found there. But Farber's image of the artist as termite also erases, almost, the question of aesthetic intention, of consciousness. This has always been the inner mystery of Elvis Presley, the mystery enclosing the grain of his voice, where the secrets are outside of words: whether, from beginning to end, he ever had a clue—whether he was, in Duncan Smith's phrase, always somehow "ex-centric to his own Elvishood." "The only credible explanation is that Elvis was from another planet, like in *Superman* or the New Testament," wrote the late Lester Bangs, who gave Elvis as much respect, suspicion, and probably more awe than any other writer: "Elvis never even had to move a muscle, not even in his face—he always, from day one till almost the very end, had that *glow*." Seeing Elvis in the flesh, on stage, in the 1970s, for the first time, Bangs said, gave him "an erection of the heart."

There was always something supernatural about him. Elvis was a force of nature. Other than that he was just a turd. A big dumb hillbilly a couple points smarter than his mule who wandered out from behind his plow one day to cut a record for his sainted mother and never came back, which he probably woulda forgot to do even if he hadn't've been whisked up. Why shouldn't one physical corpus be capable of containing these two seeming polarities simultaneously? Especially if it's from outer space.

The reason why it has been nearly impossible to credit Elvis Presley with intention beyond undifferentiated desire, which is also the reason why it remains so difficult to credit his music with meaning, is first of all social: white trash don't think. That is the premise of the Residents' *The King and Eye*, a 1990 stage show and soundtrack album, part of the conceptual-art band's revision of all American popular music. With their earlier *Stars & Hank Forever*, an LP pairing John Philip Sousa and Hank Williams, they approached both composers as lost voices, tried to make them speak, and succeeded. Played against Sousa's airs, the Residents' decomposing version of "Ramblin' Man," Williams's signature song, sounded like Williams cutting a posthumous record; it joined itself to the original, and for a moment made the original seem hedged, merely mournful. But on *The King and Eye* there is no lost voice, no new speech. All there is to hear is absence, a presence that never was: a third-rate Elvis imitator talking to a child about "the King," pretending to be trying to figure what "the King" was king of, who he was king of, or if he ever knew he was king of anything or anyone at all. Between chats the imitator bores the listener through a deadly account of seventeen hits, "All Shook Up," "Big Hunk O' Love," and so on, each of them sounding perfectly alike, like nothing—boring purposefully, like a good conceptual artist, perhaps, but not like a termite. Public Enemy said the same thing more incisively. "Elvis was a hero to most but he never meant shit to me you see," Chuck D. chanted in "Fight the Power," just warming up. "Straight up racist that sucker was/ Simple and plain."

"Plain" had to be the harder insult, but even the "most" buy the "simple." Comix artists Colin B. Morton and Chuck Death, for example (the latter in truth Jon Langford of the Mekons, the U.K.'s everlasting punk band), in panels on U2's God-sent-us-to-save-the-world-and-reinvent-rock-while-we're-at-it pretensions. In search of the Source, U2 guitarist The Edge digs up the Graceland grave while singer Bono tries to put a telephone call through to the ghost—which, incarnated as the Vegas zombie, materializes nearby, befuddled. It's the same in Jim Jarmusch's film *Mystery Train*. Young this time—and, presumably by Jarmusch's intentions, emitting far less Elvishood than any of the Elvis paintings nailed up in every room of the movie's Memphis Heartbreak Hotel—the ghost appears to an Italian woman who can't sleep for wondering why no one in town can talk about anything but a dead pop star. Naturally, the ghost doesn't know either. Hey, he was just a kid. It wasn't his fault. His pelvis was too dangerous for the masses, so he got whisked up. "I'm not a big Elvis fan," Jarmusch says. "[He was] somebody who was in the right place at the right time."

Elvis as white trash, though, will only take you so far into the mystery of why it has been so easy to deflect Elvis's music away from the realm where the music of Bob Dylan, Billie Holiday,

Prince, or even Jim Morrison takes on the aura of art, and thus invites thought. The controlling reason why it is so hard to think about Elvis aesthetically rather than sociologically is that his achievement—his cultural conquest—was seemingly so out of proportion to his means. Continents of meaning—of behavior, manners, identity, wish, and betrayal, continents of cultural politics—shifted according to certain gestures made on a television show, according to a few vocal hesitations on a handful of 45s. No one knows how to think about such a thing. Thus even such a mild comment as Camille Paglia's "Presley, a mythmaker, understood the essence of his archetypal beauty" has to pass as a writer's conceit. The idea that Elvis "understood," and thus meant, remains impossible.

Paglia is writing in *Sexual Personae: Art and Decadence from Nefertiti to Emily Dickinson*, her brutal revision of the Western cultural canon—published in 1990, though the line quoted was written well before Elvis's death. She is comparing Elvis to Byron (not a new comparison)—and both Byron and Elvis to Plato's Alcibiades and to George Villiers (1592—1628), the first Duke of Buckingham, favorite of Charles I, ambassador and crown seducer, the fate of England in his hands as he lay in the bed of the Queen of France; finally he was assassinated. ("It was such a waste. If Elvis had been killed by John, it would have at least had meaning!") Elvis is one of Paglia's "revolutionary men of beauty," an epicene and a disrupter: "Energy and beauty together are burning, godlike, destructive." With Elvis and Byron "tremendous physical energy was oddly fused with internal disorder, a revolt of the organism," Paglia says, turning the body into the body politic, making a metaphor, riffing.

Byron created the youth-cult that would sweep Elvis Presley to uncomfortable fame. In our affluent commercial culture, this man of beauty was able to ignore politics and build his empire elsewhere. A ritual function of contemporary popular culture: to parallel and purify government. . . . Mass media act as a barrier protecting politics, which would otherwise be unbalanced by the entrance of men of epochal narcissistic glamour. Today's Byronic man of beauty is a Presley who dominates the imagination, not a Buckingham who disorders a state.*

But even here Paglia slips away from attributing will to her actor. "Would sweep Presley" makes Elvis a passive, inanimate cultural object, and "a Presley" is a disembodied cultural force, not a contingent, selfish individual. And that is all too fitting, if one allows Paglia's words to silently frame the one man of beauty who did disorder the American state. Like his successor Ronald Reagan, if far more primitively, John F. Kennedy replaced politics—the considered question of what a commonality can best do with its shared space and time—with culture: what we want. Today Paglia's argument seems almost nostalgic, and idealist: Kennedy sparked the public imagination, but it was Reagan who dominated it, who owned it like property, his to do with as he wished. Culture—as an official sound-and-light show of fear and reassurance, fortune and impoverishment, just-folks mass murderers and happy families—has today so completely replaced government that there are no politics, and culture itself has lost its borders and its domain. Think of it, ponder the social fact: facing a last-place finish in the first round of the presidential elections, Prime Minister Tadeusz Mazowiecki made the desperate promise that, if elected, he would bring the Rolling Stones to Poland. A new Presley could not build an empire elsewhere because there is no elsewhere; all territory is occupied by power.

ELVIS DIES AGAIN
—Notice of cancellation of first installment of the TV show *Elvis, San Francisco Chronicle*, March 1990.

---

* There's a reverse echo of Paglia's thesis in Howard Waldrop's 1982 short story "Ike at the Mike": Dwight D. Eisenhower throws over a brilliant career in the military for jazz, becoming a master, Louis Armstrong's soulmate and comrade, while Elvis goes into politics. As a young senator eyeing the presidency, Elvis sits in the audience as aged Ike and Satchmo blow for the gods; Elvis feels a pull toward an unlived life. The story is not convincing.

ELVIS HAS LEFT THE SCHEDULE
—Notice of cancellation of second installment of *Elvis*, *San Francisco Chronicle*, May 1990.

Of course, it seemed as if all territory were occupied by power in 1956, and look what happened. What happened? Is it possible that Elvis Presley appeared on the *Ed Sullivan Show* not as a country boy eager for his big chance but as a man ready to disorder and dismember the culture that from his first moment had tried to dismember him, to fix him as a creature of resentment, rage, and fatalism, and that *had failed?* It is not possible, not according to those who revile Elvis and those like Lester Bangs who were astonished by him—and it is the impossibility of Elvis Presley as a conscious cultural agent that now buries him beneath his culture, the culture he inherited, the culture he made, and the culture that then to such a great degree remade itself according to his promises, complexities, contradictions, and defeats.* Elvis works today as a demon, and as a termite, but he works most of all in this realm of impossibility, now an idiot, now a judge.

> Me and Elvis
> Watched TV till it got late
> And we would never change the channel
> We'd use Elvis' .38
> —Human Radio, "Me and Elvis," 1990.

---

* "Even—perhaps especially—in the South, they talk about Elvis and Jesus in the same breath. There's a good reason for that. Elvis was the first public figure since Jesus that couldn't be ignored by any segment of his civilization, yet that foretold and embodied a new mode of being that would eventually dismantle the very society that was so fascinated by his presence.

"Which is perhaps the final, and most significant, of Elvis' paradoxes. In his early years Elvis was virtually apolitical, yet no one else in the '50s except Martin Luther King had as huge a political effect in the United States. Elvis singlehandedly created what came to be known as the 'youth' market, the demand for the form of music he made popular. Through being united as a market, that particular wave of youth felt the cohesion of community that became the '60s upheaval, an upheaval that all our politics since have been in reaction to, for or against." —Michael Ventura, "The Elvis in You," *LA Weekly*, 14–20 August 1987. I don't know how right Ventura is—I'm sure about his last line, not sure about his first paragraph—but it's worth noting that the enormous claims Ventura makes are in certain ways a narrowing of my own.

Elvis as judge is not the same character who blew away Robert Goulet on *The Carol Burnett Show* ("That jerk's got no heart," he said or he didn't). He's a judge who will not judge: no Solomon but an apparition, the source of values, the same Elvis that John Lennon so exquisitely professed not to believe in in "God's Song," the same Elvis whose face was on Neil Young's T-shirt on 30 September 1989, when Young sang "Rockin' in the Free World" on *Saturday Night Live*. The song—a bloody rant timed to the fall of the Berlin Wall—is a picture of the U.S.A. so bitter it takes the country right out of the free world, turns the phrase "free world" into a squalid lie. The face on the T-shirt was distant, detached, crudely sculpted, very dead, and as Young sang, the face seemed to take on the cast of the busts of Abraham Lincoln that dot the interiors in *The Manchurian Candidate*: saddened, betrayed, forced to witness every treason.

This Elvis is most obvious in Jarmusch's *Mystery Train*, looking down in every room of the hotel from his picture frames, impassive as a couple makes love or two women talk or three fugitives try to decide what to do next. Each character, in his or her way, makes an appeal to him: the young Japanese Elvis fan (her boyfriend is a purist: he favors Carl Perkins) asking for her best fuck, the gunman hoping for forgiveness. But this judge looms large only through the small-mindedness of those who conjure him up. As the hapless ghost in the Italian woman's room makes clear, this Elvis is the judge as idiot, not that the concept works. "I think it's unfortunate when people just buy a myth," says Jarmusch. "Elvis was just a guy and he got elevated to the status of almost a saint, like the Pope or something, because people can make money off that"—but as D. H. Lawrence said, "Never trust the artist. Trust the tale." "When the movie opens," said a friend, "it opens with Elvis's 'Mystery Train' "—as written, a Gothic story, Elvis driving forward against invisible doomsters to triumph, victory, a laugh—"and as the film goes on Elvis keeps moving, no one can keep up with him, no one can pin him down. So the only way they can end the movie is to cut it off, to end it with Junior

Parker's version"—the black singer's version, a slow, somber, defeated blues made in 1953, two years before Elvis sang the song—"and on that record, on the soundtrack, you hear the train stop. You can even hear the air brakes."

Dread Zeppelin's version of the idiot judge very nearly calls up the idiot Benjy from *The Sound and the Fury*, but this idiot wants to signify: he wants to judge life itself. The premises are absolute trash and the result is at once banal and grand. Led by the huge white-and-gold-suited late-period Elvis imitator Tortelvis (naturally, the final Elvis should be dessert), Dread Zeppelin is a band that plays only Led Zeppelin material to a vaguely reggae beat; the last number on their 1990 LP *Un-led-Ed* is "Moby Dick," Led Zeppelin's infamous drum solo. Opening with exploding Zeppelin chords, the piece soon finds its way into the mandated thud—and then, as what sounds like another Elvis imitator's version of "Viva Las Vegas" (Bruce Springsteen's?) comes up in the background, Tortelvis begins to *read* from *Moby-Dick*——in the slurred, drugged voice of Elvis in his notorious 19 June 1977 *Elvis in Concert* reading of "Are You Lonesome Tonight?"

It is nevertheless clear that Elvis is completely familiar with the book. Even under the cloud of dope he reads easily, with emphasis and engagement, approval and reservation. The sea, the sea, thanks to the rolling sea, its terrible depths . . . he drifts in pleasure. "Hot damn tamale, Ahab!" he shouts suddenly, then reads on, then pulls up short: "You know, I'm tired of this thing—I think he should have worded the damn thing different. Right here, look: 'When the two mates boast . . . boasts! . . . ah, that's 250 milligrams of placydils talking . . .'" He goes on, almost catching the ebb and flow of the wash as he follows the harpoon boats chasing the white whale, then slurring even more helplessly and again raising his voice: "I-I-I-I'd just like to say, I admire this Ahab character. First of all: 'And then he said to him, "I saw the opening maw of hell, with endless pains and sorrows there . . ."'" He reads again for a moment, then stops, defeat in his voice: "I've read this damn

197

book twenty-three times, Charlie,* and I still don't understand a thing." But he does: he identifies with Ahab because he is the white whale.

The Odds' Elvis is the apparition, the source of values. They are a four-piece rock 'n' roll band from Vancouver; their extraordinary "Wendy Under the Stars" began circulating on homemade cassettes in 1990, and it offered a spirit no one had ever before caught even for a moment. The music is muted, but all drama, tense, full of the secret it's about to tell; the singer is all hesitations, as if he isn't sure the time is right to let the secret go. The tune was recorded on a Sunday, in a Christian Music studio that was closed to Christians on the Sabbath; a TV played in the background, up and down—you can hear "The Star-Spangled Banner." The narrator is seventeen, a virgin; Wendy is thirty-two. They're in a room watching television, trying to understand what they're there for. She makes the first move.

> She put her finger in my ear
> But I pulled it out so I could hear
> What the newsman on the television said
> He said the King of Rock 'n' Roll was dead
> And in the spooky television light
> She said don't ever forget this night

So they leave, find a field. You can feel the cold in the singer's voice, the cold of the night, the cold of the memory: "I thought I loved her but I didn't know how / I don't love her when I see her now." But he "was fucking Wendy under the stars / The night that Elvis died / I was fucking Wendy under the stars / The night that Elvis died." When it's over, she looks him in the face.

> And in the coolness of the morning light
> She said don't ever forget this night.

---

* Dread Zeppelin are strict, academic: Charlie Hodge, Elvis's onstage servant, whose main function was to hand him scarves to toss to the crowd, can be heard giggling the words to "Are You Lonesome Tonight?" on *Elvis in Concert*.

And of course he won't: this was the night that Elvis died. Had he not, none of this would have happened—not this night. He enters the two bodies, guides them, seals the act with his presence—it's what *he* would have wanted—and the boy and the woman must rise to his promise. He's a succubus and an angel. The sense of betrayal one hears in the first punk songs about Elvis—the fury at him for not being who he said he was, the fury at his being, finally, so ordinary as to *die*—shifts now: it has taken thirteen years for the anger that powered so many good songs to change into the plainspoken awe of a better one. The singer and Wendy want Elvis to judge them; because he won't, they judge him, and they don't find him wanting. The chorus lines repeat, three times, more faintly every time; the TV comes up. Was he there? *They* were.

"Thank you, without you I'm nothing, thank you, too, without you I'm nothing, I love you, thank you, without you I'm nothing, I love you, thank you, too, without you, I'm nothing, I love you, too, Elvis—without Elvis, you're nothing."
—Madonna, closing the last show of her Blond Ambition tour, kissing her cast and crew as one by one they drop through a trapdoor in the stage, Marseille, 5 August 1990.

In Laurie Anderson's "Hiawatha," on her album *Strange Angels*, Elvis is no idiot, and he almost does judge, but he's a specter, his dim presence overshadowing any voice. The album was the attempt of a once distanced, ironic conceptual artist to leave the jargon politics of the art world and communicate without winks, to speak her necessary riddles in everyday language, to play with and submit to shared symbols, to abandon her cadenced recitations, in which the effect of every word could be mathematically calculated, to give it up for the kind of speech where any word can suggest shifts of meaning that can be neither calculated nor controlled, to sing. New York's most celebrated and severe performance artist began as Chuck Berry did in 1959, calling "Memphis, Tennessee," though speaking not as Berry's divorced father trying to reach his little girl but as a woman with a question she can't form. So she grabs for straws: starting out on the shores of Gitche Gumee, she calls up Captain Midnight, JFK, Geronimo, Marilyn Monroe, as if it were Elvis who by the force of his personality has given all of these old symbols their resonance. And as if now they are only reflections of him, all chronology dissolved in the mythology of symbolism, she goes back to the source.

> And I said: Hello Operator
> Get me Memphis Tennessee
> And she said: I know who you're tryin'
> To call darlin And he's not home
> He's been away
> But you can hear him on the airwaves
> He's howlin at the moon
> Yeah this is your country station
> And honey this one's for you

"The King sings Love Me Tender," Anderson whispers, but she puts a remarkable verse between that line and the verse quoted above, sung from an infinite distance, Elvis Presley speaking from so far away it seems unnatural that any words from Anderson could follow his, these: "So good night ladies / And good night gentlemen / Keep those card and letters coming / And please don't call again." It's the plea of a judge judging all those who wait outside the locked doors of his court: *Why do you talk about me as if I'm still here?*

"I don't always agree with your communistic diatribes," said Elvis Presley at the June 17 CBGB *Village Voice* Strike Fund Benefit, "but I believe in your right to print them." Then the King tore through "Love Me Tender" and "Jailhouse Rock" before stopping to toss keys to a Lincoln, Caddy, Mercedes, Jaguar, and Chevy out to an eager, screaming audi-

200   ence . . .   —*Village Voice*, 3 July 1990.

Michel Delsol, photo of Mark Alan Stamaty as Elvis Presley for the *Village Voice*, 1990.

On *The Last Temptation of Elvis* it's Holly Johnson, once famed as lead singer for Hype of '84 Frankie Goes to Hollywood ("Relax" on the soundtrack to *Body Double* was as close as they got), who sings "Love Me Tender." Like a lot of the people on the discs, he sings as if he wants Elvis's approval. A lot of the other people sing as if they want to see what they can get away with: "I have a need / To overfeed," says Vivian Stanshall as he kicks off "No Room to Rhumba in a Sports Car," and Pop Will Eat Itself even samples Public Enemy's "Elvis was a hero to most . . ." to end their frantically obsessive cutup of "Rock-a-Hula-Baby." But regardless of style, two questions seem to energize every performer: what would Elvis think of this? Do I care?

The whole project is of course a dare: the singers daring Elvis, daring his most degraded, greatest-shit material to give something

201

back; Elvis daring the singers to find life in songs where so often he found only humiliation. The result is a fabulous cultural anarchy, shaped song by song by the complex of worship and resentment all fans carry. The set exults in the confusion its premise produces. No performance implies any other. There's no way to predict what anyone will have to say. Cath Carroll and Steve Albini's jagged "King Creole" is followed by Aaron Neville's "Young and Beautiful," sung with daunting modesty to a nightclub crowd that clinks and chatters as if Neville is an opening act, which is itself followed by Stanshall's absurdist "No Room to Rhumba." Robert Plant's "Let's Have a Party" bleeds despair into the happy lyric, then revs up for the Rockabilly Hall of Fame and makes it home (Elvis didn't even try); the Pogues' "Got a Lot o' Livin' to Do," next up, is equally bent on a hall of shame. *The Last Temptation of Elvis* stops you right here, anywhere, makes you wonder: what's going on? What would Elvis think of this?

Aaron Neville sings slowly, delicately—but the way the great soul singer keeps saying Elvis's name to his audience, to himself, is so ethereal it's scary. You can't tell what he means, what he's trying to say, and you're not sure he could either, except that the performance is telling you: it's a prayer aimed straight at the song's first singer. You could have stayed young and beautiful forever, Neville seems to say, and I too, if only you'd never stopped singing as clearly as you sang this song—*why didn't you?* Wrapped inside this fan's devotion is the most gentle damning Elvis Presley will ever receive. Can it be an accident that in "Pharaoh's Palace (Memphis, 1988)," one of three poems about Graceland in David Wojahn's *Mystery Train*, the same song takes another artist to the same depths?

> We weave
>   Down the sidewalk
> to the grave, the clumsy epitaph his Daddy wrote.
>   A woman walks off
> sobbing to herself. Her husband in cowboy boots,
>   face a patch

of oily sores, follows her shaking his fist, slaps her twice
  and tells her *Goddamn you, shut up*.

He drags her off by the arm, but still she's
  wailing, sorrowfully
crouched on a bench. On the parking lot loudspeaker
  he's performing
"Young and Beautiful." On the two-lane headed home, we stop
  at a house claimed

by kudzu and grass, barn and house collapsed, wood a uniform
  gray, windows shuttered.
Evening comes on: we walk a path to a family plot,
  a hornet's nest patching
a single marker proclaiming no name, only HERE US
  O LORD IN R SORROW

In the revel of *The Last Temptation*, Elvis becomes a magic mirror, then a lost reflection. As the performers turn Elvis into a judge of their music, of themselves, they themselves become judges, and judge him—and this makes them feel free. The story seems brand new. Any song—any Elvis—seems possible.

This is, perhaps, where the termite runs out of barriers: in the sky, or in a house fallen down around itself, the wood already rotten. This is Elvis Presley without music; without history; without a body, neither bopper nor corpse. But all of that is somehow, for an instant, replaced in Neville's "Young and Beautiful," in Wojahn's memory of once hearing the song, or for that matter in the way Elvis sings it in the last shots of *Jailhouse Rock*. For just a second you can feel how far Elvis has really traveled in our culture, and how far he really traveled on his own. You can sense where he came from, why he left, why he came back, and where he ended up.

The story shrinks then, down to the size of your favorite song, whatever it is—down to the size of whatever mystery *it* contains, whatever it was that made you like it then, and like it now.

Citations

Books are listed by author or editor; narrative videos by director; articles in periodicals by author, except where no author is given, in which case articles are listed by publication and then title; individual recordings and music videos are listed by performer; movies, television shows, and various-artists recordings are listed by title.

Adorno, Theodor. *Minima Moralia: Reflections from Damaged Life* (1951), trans. G. F. N. Jephcott. London: Verso, 1978. No. 36, "The Health unto Death," p. 59.
Adventures of Ford Fairlane, The. Dir. Renny Harlin. 20th Century-Fox, 1990.
Anderson, Laurie. "Hiawatha," from *Strange Angels* (Warner Bros., 1989).
Art Bears. *The World As It Is Today* (RēRecords, U.K., 1981).
Association fédérative générale des étudiants de Strasbourg/Internationale situationniste. *De la misère en milieu étudiant, considérée sous ses aspects économique, politique, psychologique, sexuel et notamment intellectuel et de quelques moyens pour y remédier.* Strasbourg: AFGES, 1966. Reprinted Paris: Champ Libre, 1977. Trans. Situationist International as *Ten Days That Shook the University: The Situationists at Strasbourg.* London: SI, 1967.
Atwood, Margaret. *The Handmaid's Tale.* New York: Houghton Mifflin, 1986.

Bad Influence. Dir. Curtis Hanson. Columbia Pictures, 1990.
Ball, Hugo. *Flight Out of Time: A Dada Diary* (1927, *Die Flucht aus der Zeit*), ed. John Elderfield, trans. Ann Raimes. New York: Viking, 1974. P. 67, entry for 16 June 1916.
Bangs, Lester. "Where Were You When Elvis Died?" (1977), and "Notes for Review of Peter Guralnick's *Lost Highway*, 1980," in *Psychotic Reactions and Carburetor Dung*, ed. Greil Marcus. New York: Knopf, 1987. Pp. 215, 327, 329–331.
Barson, Michael. *Rip It Up! Postcards from the Heyday of Rock 'n' Roll.* New York: Pantheon, 1989.
Brown, A. Whitney, "The Big Picture," *Saturday Night Live*, 9 May 1987, NBC. A different version appears in Brown, "Races vs. Races," in *The Big Picture: An American Commentary.* New York: HarperPerennial, 1991. P. 142.
Brown, James. "Cig Vicious" (on Dennis Leary). New Musical Express, 11 August 1990. P. 21.
Burnette, Billy Joe. "Welcome Home Elvis" (Gusto-Starday, 1977). Burnette is the son of Johnny Burnette, who like Elvis worked for Crown Electric in Memphis and was part of the very early Memphis rockabilly milieu. So much for bloodlines.
Burse, Charlie. "Shorty the Barber" (1950), on *Sun Records—The Blues Years, 1950–1956* (Sun/Charly, U.K., 1984). Burse was the second artist recorded by Sam Phillips, though the results were originally unreleased. See also *Charlie Burse—James De Berry: Complete Recordings in Chronological Order (1939)* (Old Tramp/Blues Record Centre, Holland, 1989).
Butthole Surfers. "The Revenge of Anus Parsley," from *Butthole Surfers* (Alternative Tentacles, 1983).
Cave, Nick, and the Bad Seeds. *The Firstborn Is Dead* (Homestead, U.S., Mute, U.K., 1985).
Coasters. "Framed" and "Riot in Cell Block No. 9" (Spark, 1954, originally released as by the Robins).

Cohn, Nik. *Awopbopaloobop Alopbamboom: Pop from the Beginning* (1969, as *Pop from the Beginning*, U.K., and *Rock from the Beginning*, U.S.). London: Paladin, 1972. Excerpt in *Ball the Wall: Nik Cohn in the Age of Rock*. London: Picador, 1989.

———. *I Am Still the Greatest Says Johnny Angelo*. London: Secker & Warburg, 1967. Excerpt in *Ball the Wall*.

———. *King Death*. New York: Harcourt Brace Jovanovich, 1975. Excerpt in *Ball the Wall*.

———. with Guy Peellaert. *Rock Dreams* (1973). New York: Rogner & Bernhard/Random House, 1982.

Cool It Reba. "Money Fall Out the Sky," from *Money Fall Out the Sky* (Hannibal, 1982).

Corboy, Thomas. *Rock 'n' Roll Disciples*. Monticello Productions, 1985.

Cortez, Diego, ed. *Private Elvis*. Stuttgart: FEY, 1978. P. 11 and passim.

Cortinas. "Defiant Pose" (Step-Forward, U.K., 1978). Color reproduction of sleeve in *Walk Away Renée: An ABC of the Work of Hipgnosis*. New York: Hipgnosis/Paper Tiger/A&W Visual Library, 1978. P. 137.

Costello, Elvis. Unpublished collage, 1989.

Cotten, Lee. *All Shook Up: Elvis Day-by-Day, 1954–1977*. Ann Arbor: Pierian Press, 1985.

———, with Howard A. DeWitt. *Jailhouse Rock: The Bootleg Records of Elvis Presley, 1970–1983*. Ann Arbor: Pierian Press, 1983.

Crime Story. Prod. Michael Mann. NBC, 1986–88.

Days and Nights of Molly Dodd, The. Prod. Bernie Brillstein and Jay Tarses. Lifetime, 25 May 1990.

De Barbin, Lucy and Dary Matera. *Are You Lonesome Tonight? The Untold Story of Elvis Presley's One True Love—and the Child He Never Knew*. New York: Villard, 1987.

Dodge, Jim. *Not Fade Away*. New York: Atlantic Monthly Press, 1987.

Dread Zeppelin. "Moby Dick," from *Un-led-Ed* (I.R.S., 1990).

Dundy, Elaine. *Elvis and Gladys*. New York: Macmillan, 1985. Pp. 18, 26, 229.

Eggleston, William. Uncollected photographs of Graceland, 1983. See Martin Filler, "Elvis Presley's Graceland: An American Shrine," *House & Garden*, March 1984, pp. 140–46, and Greil Marcus, "William Eggleston's View of Graceland: The Absence of Elvis," *Artforum*, March 1984, pp. 70–72.

Elvis. Prod. James Parriot. ABC, 1990.

Elvis Bourbon bottle. McCormick Distilling Co., Weston, MO. About 1980. Plays "Love Me Tender."

Elvis Classics: R & B Tunes Covered by Elvis Presley (P-Vine, Japan, 1989). Original versions of "Elvis songs," including "Hound Dog" by Willie Mae Thornton (1953), "When It Rains, It Really Pours" by Billy "The Kid" Emerson (1955), and twenty-four others.

Elvis: What Happened? See West, Red, et al.

Factory Sample, A (Factory, U.K., 1978). Double EP with sticker insert, including recordings by Joy Division, the Durutti Column, Cabaret Voltaire, and John Dowie.

Farber, Manny. "White Elephant and Termite Art" (1962), in *Negative Space: Manny Farber on the Movies*. New York: Praeger, 1971. Pp. 135–36.

Flanagan, Bill. "Bono," from *Written in My Soul: Rock's Great Songwriters Talk About Creating Their Music*. Chicago: Contemporary Books, 1986. Pp. 415–16.

Fox, William Price. *Dixiana Moon*. New York: Viking, 1981.

———. *Ruby Red*. New York: Lippincott, 1971.

Frith, Simon. *Sound Effects: Youth, Leisure, and the Politics of Rock 'n' Roll*. New York: Pantheon, 1981. On Elvis and the "grain of the voice," p. 165.

Gaiman, Neil and Terry Pratchett. *Good Omens: The Nice and Accurate Prophecies of Agnes Nutter, Witch*. New York: Workman, 1990. Pp. 112–13.

Goldman, Albert. *Elvis*. New York: McGraw-Hill, 1981. At one time subtitled "With the Memories of the American People."

Gray, Christopher, ed. and trans. *Leaving the 20th Century: The Incomplete Work of the Situationist International*. U.K.: Free Fall, 1974. Pp. 10, 31–32. Designed by Jamie Reid.

Guralnick, Peter. *Lost Highway: Journeys & Arrivals of American Musicians* (1979). New York: Harper & Row, 1989.

Heartfield, John. *Hurrah, die Butter ist alle!* Originally published in *A-I-Z-* (Prague), 19 December 1935. See Wieland Herzefelde, *John Heartfield: Leben und Werk*. Dresden: Veb Verlag Kunst, 1962 and 1971. Fig. 195.

Henley, Don. "If Dirt Were Dollars," from *The End of the Innocence* (Geffen, 1989).

Hopkins, Jerry. *Elvis*. New York: Simon and Schuster, 1971.

Human Radio. "Me and Elvis," from *Human Radio* (Columbia, 1990).

Kent, Nick. "Roy Orbison: The Last Interview." *The Face*, February 1989. P. 39.

Knight, Sonny. See Smith, Joseph C.

Last Temptation of Elvis, The: Songs from His Movies (New Musical Express, U.K., 1990).

Ledbetter, James. "Media Blitz." Village Voice, 28 August 1990. P. 9.

Lee Spike. "Eddie" (interview with Eddie Murphy). *Spin*, October 1990. P. 34.

Lennonburger. Page in "This Could Happen to *Your* City! The Northern California Underground Uprising of '82," booklet included in *Maximum Rock n Roll Presents Not So Quiet on the Western Front* (Alternative Tentacles, U.S., Faulty Products, U.K., 1982).

Lewis, Jerry Lee. *Classic Jerry Lee Lewis* (Bear Family, Germany, 1988). Material recorded for the Sun label, 1956–63, on 8 CDs.

———, and Friends. *Duets* (Sun, 1979).

Living Colour. "Elvis is Dead," from *Time's Up* (Epic, 1990).

Lowry, Ray. "Elvisburgers" cartoon, in *This Space to Let*. London: Abacus/Sphere, 1986. Originally in *New Musical Express*, 8 January 1983.

McClanahan, Ed. "Little Enis: An Ode on the Intimidations of Mortality," from *Famous People I Have Known*. New York: Farrar Straus Giroux, 1985. Pp. 115–56 and frontispiece.

McKee, Margaret and Fred Chisenall. *Beale Black & Blue*. Baton Rouge: Louisiana State University Press, 1981. Pp. 94–95. For more on a young Elvis on Beale Street, see Stanley Booth, "Phineas Newborn Jr.–Fascinating Changes." *Village Voice*, 18 July 1989, *Rock & Roll Quarterly*, p. 19. Booth on Memphis guitarist Calvin Newborn at the Flamingo Room, previously the Alta Hotel Men's Improvement Club at Hernando and Beale: "Calvin . . . had become such a showman that Flamingo owner Clifford Miller booked guitar battles. 'You'd have guitar players to come in and battle me,' Calvin has said, 'like Pee Wee Crayton and Gatemouth Brown, and I was battlin' out there, tearin' they behind up, 'cause I was dancin', playin', puttin' on a show, slidin' across the flo'. . . .' One night, probably in late 1952, a teenaged white boy 'came in there, didn't have on any shoes, barefooted, and asked me if he could play my guitar. I didn't want to let him, I don't usually—I didn't know him from Adam. I'd never seen him before. In fact, he was the only white somebody in the club. He made sure he won that one. He sang "You Ain't Nothin' But a Hound Dog" and shook his hair—see, at the time I had my hair processed, and I'd shake it down in my face—he tore the house *up*. And tore the strings off my guitar so I couldn't follow him.' " Even if the first recording of "Hound Dog," by Willie Mae Thornton, was not released until 1953 . . .

Medallions. "The Letter" (Dootone, 1955).

Mekons. "Memphis, Egypt," from *The Mekons Rock 'n' Roll* (A&M/TwinTone, U.S., Blast First, U.K., 1989).

Menand, Louis. "Life in the Stone Age." *New Republic*, 7 & 14 January 1991. P. 39.

Michasiw, K. I. "The King Is Dead, Long Live the King." Unpublished paper. Courtesy Michasiw and Jonathan Kanana.

Mishima. Dir. Paul Schrader. Filmlink. 1985.

Morton, Colin B. and Chuck Death. *Great Pop Things.* "Expresso Bongo! U2 Part 2." *LA Weekly*, 15–21 June 1990. P. 105.

Myles, Alannah. "Black Velvet" (Atlantic, 1989).

Mystery Train. Dir. Jim Jarmusch. Orion Classics. 1989.

Nesmith, Michael. *Elephant Parts.* Pacific Arts Video. 1981.

Nightingales. "Elvis, the Last Ten Days" (Cherry Red, U.K., 1981).

Nixon, Mojo and Skid Roper. "Elvis Is Everywhere," from *Bo-Day-Shus!!!* (Enigma, 1987).

O'Brien, Glenn. "Like Art: Surrealism with Everything On It." *Artforum*, April 1986. P. 7.

Odds. "Wendy Under the Stars," from *By the Seat of Our Pants* (unreleased demo cassette, 1990). New version on Odds, *Neopolitan* (Zoo/BMG, 1991).

Paglia, Camille. *Sexual Personae: Art and Decadence from Nefertiti to Emily Dickinson.* New Haven and London: Yale, 1990. Pp. 362, 364.

Panter, Gary. *Invasion of the Elvis Zombies.* New York: Raw Books, and Valencia, Spain: Arrebato Editorial, 1984.

Parsons, Bill (Bobby Bare). "The All American Boy" (Fraternity, 1958).

Paterson, Donald. *Elvis in Egypt.* See Susan Subtle Dintenfass, "Elvis in Egypt," *California Magazine*, November 1989. Pp. 103–7.

Pattison, Robert. *The Triumph of Vulgarity: Rock Music in the Mirror of Romanticism.* New York: Oxford, 1987.

Penguins. "Earth Angel (Will You Be Mine)" (Dootone, 1954). Recorded by Elvis in Germany c. 1958–60; see *A Golden Celebration*.

Pet Shop Boys. "Always on My Mind," from *Introspection* (Manhattan, 1988).

Pic of the Poseurs: Magazine for Modern Youth. Includes "Presleyburger Shock," anonymous text by Ray Holme and Joby Hooligan. London, 1977. Courtesy Jon Savage.

Pratt, Linda Ray. "Elvis, or the Ironies of a Southern Identity," from *Elvis: Images and Fancies*, ed. Jac L. Tharpe. Jackson: University Press of Mississippi, 1979. Pp. 45, 51.

Presley, Elvis. "Blue Moon of Kentucky (alternate take," recorded 1954, on *The Complete Sun Sessions* (RCA, 1987).

———. *Elvis for Everyone* (RCA, 1965).

———. *Elvis' "Greatest Shit!!"* (Dog Vomit, 1982).

———. *Elvis Is Back!* (RCA, 1960).

———. *Elvis: One Night with You.* HBO, 1985. Music Media video, 1985. One of two complete performances with small combo for 1968 comeback TV special.

———. *Elvis Presley Sings Leiber and Stoller* (RCA CD, 1991). Includes "Hound Dog,"

"Love Me" (both 1956), "Jailhouse Rock," "Treat Me Nice," "(You're So Square) Baby I Don't Care," and "Loving You" (all 1957), "Santa Claus Is Back in Town" and "Don't" (both 1958).

————. Letter to President Richard M. Nixon (19 December 1970). See Fred L. Worth and Steve D. Tamerius, *Elvis: His Life from A to Z*. Chicago: Contemporary Books, 1988. P. 141.

————. "Long Black Limousine," from *From Elvis in Memphis* (RCA, 1969).

————. "Memories," from *Elvis TV Special* (RCA, 1968). See also *Elvis: One Night with You*.

————. "My Happiness," recorded 1953, on *The Great Performances* (RCA, 1990).

————. "Tryin' to Get to You," recorded 1968, on *Elvis: One Night with You*. See also *A Golden Celebration* (RCA, 1985).

————. "Young and Beautiful," recorded 1957, on *A Date with Elvis* (RCA, 1963).

Presley, Priscilla Beaulieu with Sandra Harmon. *Elvis and Me*. New York: Putnam's, 1985.

Psychic Reader (Santa Rosa, CA). "Elvis, the Channel" (or, "Knock, Knock, Who's There?"). April 1987, P. 26.

Public Enemy. "Fight the Power," on *Fear of a Black Planet* (Def Jam/Columbia, 1990). First used in the 1989 Spike Lee film, *Do the Right Thing*, and released as "Fight the Power (Music from 'Do the Right Thing')" (Motown, 1989).

Reid, Jamie. *Up They Rise: The Incomplete Works of Jamie Reid*. London: Faber & Faber, 1987. Pp. 8–9, 90.

Residents. *The King and Eye* (Enigma, 1990).

————. "Ramblin' Man," on *Stars & Hank Forever: The American Composers Series— Volume II* (Ralph, 1986). *Volume I* was *George & James*, as in Gershwin and Brown.

Robins. See Coasters.

Savage, Jon. Anonymous text from the Jamie Reid Collection, Victoria & Albert Museum, London. Quoted in Vermorel, Fred and Judy. *Sex Pistols: The Inside Story* (1978). London: Omnibus, 3rd rev. ed., 1987. Pp. 140–41. See also Reid, *Up They Rise*. P. 93.

Sex Pistols. "C'mon Everybody" (Virgin, U.K., 1979). Second Sex Pistols single featuring the posthumous Sid Vicious.

————. "Satellite"/"Holidays in the Sun" (Virgin, U.K., 1977). The "Nice Drawing," as the Jamie Reid image on the "Satellite" sleeve was called, first appeared in Reid's unpublished "Cat Book," a satire on suburban death culture; then in *You Can't Judge a Book by Looking at the Cover*, in 1973, an attack on planned suburbs; then in Gray, *Leaving the 20th Century*, and finally on the Sex Pistols' rant against South London suburbia. See Reid, *Up They Rise*. Pp. 8–9.

Siouxsie and the Banshees. "Mittageisen (for John Heartfield)" (Polydor, U.K. and Germany, 1979).

Situationist International. See Association fédérative générale des étudiants de Strasbourg.

Smith, Joseph C. *The Day the Music Died*. New York: Grove, 1981.

————. "But Officer" (Aladdin, 1953).

————. "Confidential"/"Jail Bird" (Vita, Dot, 1956).

————. "If You Want This Love" (Aura, 1964). This and the three preceding recordings can be found on Sonny Knight, *"Confidential"* (Mr R&B, Sweden).

Sonic Youth. "Tunic (Song for Karen)," from *Goo* (DGC, 1990).

Straw, Syd. "Listening to Elvis," from the anthology *Luxury Condos Coming to Your Neighborhood Soon* (Coyote, 1985). Accompaniment by the Del-Lords; composition by Scott Kempner.

Thompson, Charles C. II and James P. Cole. *The Death of Elvis Presley: What* Really *Happened*. New York: Delacorte, 1991. Pp. 24–26.

Thornton, Willie Mae with Kansas City Bill [Johnny Otis] and Orchestra. "Hound Dog" (Peacock, 1953). See also *Elvis Classics*.

Tosches, Nick. *Country: The Biggest Music in America*. New York: Stein & Day, 1977. Pp. 39–49.

———. *Hellfire: The Jerry Lee Lewis Story* (1982). New York: Delta, 2d. rev. ed., 1989.

Twin Peaks. Prod. Mark Frost and David Lynch. ABC, 3 May 1990.

U2. "Elvis Presley and America," from *The Unforgettable Fire* (Island, 1984).

Vaneigem, Raoul. *Traité de savoir-vivre à l'usage des jeunes générations* (1967). Paris: Gallimard, 1981. P. 19. Trans. Donald Nicholson-Smith as *The Revolution of Everyday Life*. Seattle: Left Bank Books, and London: Rebel Press, 1983. P. 15.

Vaughn, Ben. "In the Presence of Legends: Charlie Feathers." *The Bob* (Wilmington, DE), Summer 1990. P. 7.

Ventura, Michael. "The Elvis in You." *LA Weekly*, 14–20 August 1987. P. 20.

———. "Hear That Long Snake Moan," from *Shadow Dancing in the U.S.A.* Los Angeles: J. P. Tarcher/New York: St. Martin's, 1985. Pp. 152–56.

Vermorel, Fred and Judy. *Starlust: The Secret Fantasies of Fans*. London: W. H. Allen, 1985.

Waldrop, Howard. "Ike at the Mike" (1982), in *Strange Things in Close Up: The Nearly Complete Howard Waldrop*. London: Legend/Arrow, 1989. Pp. 49–64.

Walker, Alice. "Nineteen Fifty-five," in *You Can't Keep a Good Woman Down*. New York: Harcourt Brace Jovanovich, 1981. Pp. 3–20.

Wark, McKenzie. "Elvis, Listen to the Loss." *Art & Text* No. 31, December 1988–February 1989 (Australia). Pp. 27–28.

West, Red, Sonny West, Dave Hebler as told to Steve Dunleavy. *Elvis: What Happened?* New York: Ballantine, 1977.

Wild at Heart. Dir. David Lynch. Polygram/Propaganda Films. 1990.

Wojahn, David. "Elvis Moving a Small Cloud: The Desert Near Las Vegas, 1976," and "Pharaoh's Palace (Memphis, 1988)," from *Mystery Train*. Pittsburgh: University of Pittsburgh Press, 1990. Pp. 39, 59–61. Other poems in Wojahn's history of rock 'n' roll include "W.C.W. Watching Presley's Second Appearance on 'The Ed Sullivan Show,' Mercy Hospital, Newark, 1956," "The Trashmen Shaking Hands with Hubert Humphrey at the Opening of Apache Plaza Shopping Center, Suburban Minneapolis, August 1962," and "Francis Ford Coppola and Anthropologist Interpreter Teaching Gartewienna Tribesmen to Sing 'Light My Fire,' Philippine Jungle, 1978."

Wolcott, James. "Elvis: Shot by His Own Harpoon." *Village Voice*, 17 March 1981. P. 57.

Wolfe, Charles. Unpublished research on school children and Elvis, presented at seminar "Elvis Is Everywhere," Southern Festival of Books, Nashville, 13 October 1990.

Wylie, Pete/Wah! "The Story of the Blues, Part One and Part Two" (Eternal/WEA, U.K., 1982).

X. "Back 2 the Base," from *Wild Gift* (Slash, 1981).

Young, Neil. "Rockin' in the Free World," *Saturday Night Live*, NBC, 30 September 1989. See also Young, *Freedom* (Reprise, 1989).

Zevon, Warren. "Jesus Mentioned," from *The Envoy* (Elektra/Asylum, 1982).

212

Acknowledgments

From "Mystery Train" to "Can't Help Falling in Love" to "Long Black Limousine," for Jenny, Emily, and Cessie, first and last.

Many people helped start this book and keep it going, with rumors, mailings, clippings, tape recordings, radio shows, conferences, books, art works, and countless breachings of the walls of disbelief; for all that and more, I thank Laurie Anderson, Scott Arundale, John Bakke of Memphis State University, Bill Barminski, Andrew Baumer, Adam Block, Dale and Steve Block, Boff of Chumbawamba, Stanley Booth, Liz Bordow, Barbara Carr, Kent Carroll, Shari Cavin and Russell Morris of the Cavin-Morris Gallery, Bryan Chambliss, Jay Orr, and Martha Starin of the Tennessee Humanities Council, Jill and Paul Chesler, Robert Christgau, Gary Ciccarelli, Michael Conen, Elvis Costello, Paul de Angelis, Anthony DeCurtis, Michael Delsol, Susan Subtle Dintenfass, M. Dung of KFOG-FM, Michael Ferguson, Geraldine Fink, Tony Fitzpatrick, Leanne Friedman (who embarrassed and thrilled everyone in our fourth-grade class when she went to see Elvis at the Cow Palace in 1955), Simon Frith, Michael Goodwin, Lexy Green, Tom Greenhalgh and Jon Langford of the Mekons, Peter Guralnick, Howard Hampton, Lisa Hanauer, Bill Holdship, Christian Höller, House of Love and Scott Kane of KALX-FM, John Howell, Robert Hull, Jonathan Kahana, Elizabeth Kaye, the late Marion Keisker, my typist Nancy Laleav, Marilyn Laverty, S. K. List, Ray Lowry, Tom Luddy, Joni Mabe, Bill Marcus, Daniel Marcus, Eleanore and Gerald Marcus, Steve Marcus, Dave Marsh, Sharyn McCrumb, Tony McGregor, K. I. Michasiw, Jim Miller, Joyce Millman, Bruce Miroff, Toru Mitsui, John Morthland, Craig Northey of the Odds, Michael Ochs, Chris Ohman, Gary Panter, Linda Ray Pratt, Steve Propes, Jamie Reid, Ger Rijff, Stephen Ronan, Cynthia Rose, Sandra Rosenzweig, Luc Sante, Mike Saunders, Jon Savage, Mark Shipper, R J Smith, Lang Thompson, Nick Tosches, Michael Trossman, Ken Tucker, Jan van Gestel, Lin van Heuit, Michael Ventura, Fred Vermorel, Anne Wagner, Alice Walker, Ed Ward, McKenzie Wark, Steve Wasserman, Katharina Weingartner, the late Bill Whitehead, John Wiener, David Wojahn, Charles Wolfe, and Peter Wood.

For their editorial spark and guidance, my thanks go to David Frankel, Ingrid Sischy, Robin Cembalest, Ida Panicelli, Anthony Korner, Charles Miller, Andrea Codrington, and Jane Ryan Beck at *Artforum*; John Burks at *City*; the late Lester Bangs and Charles Auringer at *Creem*; Kyle D. Young at the *Journal of Country Music*; Nancy Friedman, Janet Duckworth, and Jon Carroll at *New West* and *California*; Barbara Downey Landau and Jann Wenner at *Rolling Stone*; Bart Bull at *Spin*; Jon Wozencroft at *Touch*; M. Mark at the *Voice Literary Supplement*; and, month after month with never a demurer, Doug Simmons at the *Village Voice*. Pieces in this book that first appeared under their aegis, often in very different or abbreviated form, are:

"Blue Hawaii"—*Rolling Stone*, 22 September 1977
"Jungle Music"—*City*, 2 April 1975, and *Creem*, July 1975
"King Death"—*Rolling Stone*, 23 October 1975 (as "Applause for the Angel of Death")
"Duets"—*Rolling Stone*, 17 May 1979
"Tales from the Crypt"—*Rolling Stone*, 14 December 1978

"The Myth Behind the Truth Behind the Legend"—*Voice Literary Supplement*, December 1981 (as "Lies About Elvis, Lies About Us")

"The Road Away from Graceland"—*New West*, 10 March 1980 (as "That Long, Lonesome Road")

"A View of Graceland: The Absence of Elvis"—*Artforum*, March 1984 (as "William Eggleston's View of Graceland: The Absence of Elvis")

"The Last Breakfast"—*Artforum*, February 1985 (as "The Last Supper")

"The King of Rhythm & Blues"—*New West*, June 1981 (as "Take the Money and Run")

"Good Book on Elvis Published: Shocking Truth Revealed"—*Journal of Country Music*, 1986, Vol. XI, No. 1 (as "Playing House with Elvis")

"Ten Years After: Death on the Installment Plan"—*Spin*, August 1987 (as "Antihero")

"The Man Who Wasn't Elvis"—*California*, April 1982 (as "Days of Doom")

"Emanations, Sightings, Disappearances, or A Seance of Eighteen Mediums"—entries through 1989 appeared in various installments of "Real Life Rock Top Ten," *Village Voice*, 18 March 1986, 10 February 1987, 25 August 1987, 1 March 1988, 29 November 1988, 21 February 1989, 18 April 1989, 18 July 1989, 14 November 1989, and 12 December 1989

"A Corpse in Your Mouth: Adventures of a Metaphor, or Modern Cannibalism"—*Touch*, Spring 1986 (as "The Corpse Metaphor: Ritual Is Where You Find It")

"Still Dead: Elvis Presley Without Music"—*Artforum*, September 1990

At Doubleday I was lucky to receive the counsel and enthusiasm of Martha Levin, David Gernert, Wendy Goldman, Kathy Trager, Julie Duquet, Marysarah Quinn, and especially, day by day, Paul Bresnick; at Penguin, Jonathan Riley. And Wendy Weil and Jennifer Smith of the Wendy Weil Agency, with Anthony Goff in London, made everything easy.

216

Permissions

Index

(References to illustrations are italicized.)

223

225